CLEAR THE DECK!

AIRCRAFT CARRIER ACCIDENTS OF WORLD WAR II

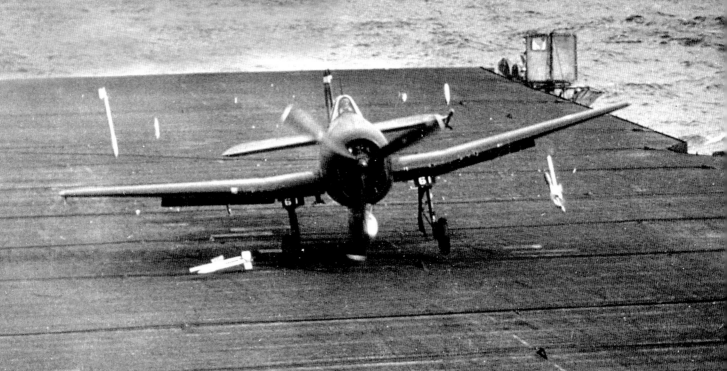

CORY GRAFF

Edited by Nicholas A. Veronico

Designed by Connie Nordrum

ISBN-13 978-1-58007-119-2

39966 Grand Avenue
North Branch, MN 55056 USA
(651) 277-1400 or (800) 895-4585
www.specialtypress.com

Printed in China

Library of Congress Cataloging-in-Publication Data

Graff, Cory, 1971-
  Clear the deck! : naval aviation incidents and accidents of World War II / by Cory Graff.
    p. cm.
  ISBN 978-1-58007-119-2
  1. World War, 1939-1945--Aerial operations, American. 2. United States. Navy--Aviation. 3. World War, 1939-1945--Aerial operations, Japanese. 4. Japan. Kaigun--Aviation. I. Title.
    D790.3.G73 2008
    940.54'5--dc22
                                2008001955

On the Cover:
As a Hellcat wallows after a wave-off, the LSO sprints across the Cabot's deck to get out of the way of the imminent catastrophic crash. Commonly, the LSO would dive into a net situated below his platform on the port side of the deck. However, in this case the VF-29 fighter, clawing for air, appears to be headed that way, calling for an alternate escape plan. (National Museum of Naval Aviation)

Title Page:
A load of rockets bounces loose from a Hellcat during a hard landing on Essex on December 19, 1944. (National Archives)

Back Cover (Clockwise from top left):
An Avenger plunges into the water off the port side of a carrier after dragging its wing across the deck. The bomber was most likely caught in a torque roll following a wave off, the pilot adding power to its big Wright R-2600 Cyclone radial engine too quickly to get out of a jam. Now, as some pilots were fond of saying, he and his crew are "going swimming." (National Archives)

"Arky" Snowden loses the tail of his F6F-3 while landing aboard Belleau Wood in August 1943. The front two-thirds of the fighter scooted between the ship's stacks and dropped to the water. Only the plane's tail and right landing gear stayed on the deck. A destroyer picked up the pilot just as the ripped-apart Hellcat slipped under the waves. (National Museum of Naval Aviation)

In an explosion of splinters, the engine of an F4U-1 Corsair rips loose on the deck of Charger in May 1944. The plane came in long, missed the wires, and hit the crash barrier while in mid-bounce, flipping completely over. The plane was assigned to VOF-1. (U.S. Navy via Peter Bowers)

Distributed in the UK and Europe by:

Midland Publishing
4 Watling Drive
Hinckley LE10 3EY, England
Tel: 01455 233 747 Fax: 01455 233 737
www.midlandcountiessuperstore.com

Table of Contents

Acknowledgments:

Most of the photographs in this volume were taken "on the job" by U.S. Navy and Marine Corps photographers. The images were found in various institutions, including the National Archives, the Naval Historical Center, and the National Museum of Naval Aviation. Other photos came from Northrop Grumman, The Museum of Flight, and the private collections of Navy and Marine Corps flyers. Special thanks to Holly Reed, M. Hill Goodspeed, Edwin Finney, Lynn McDonald, Paul Madden, Peter Bowers, Dick Rainforth, Norm Taylor, Shauna Simon, Shawn Chamberlain, Patrick Kam, and Katherine Williams. Also, thanks to Nicholas A. Veronico, Susan Helberg, Karin Hill, and Katie Sonmor of Specialty Press, who helped make this book a reality.

CHAPTER ONE

PRELUDE TO WAR

Flying from a ship was a perilous pursuit. There were a hundred or more ways to bungle it up. And one small mistake meant a flyer would probably be burned, bludgeoned, crushed, or drowned. Some airmen morbidly mused that an unlucky pilot might even experience some unknowable combination of these tortures before succumbing to the ominous depths.

So in 1910, when the United States Navy came calling, hoping to find a brave soul who would set out from a ship in his rickety aeroplane, many famous flyers had little trouble generating a dispassionate rejection. Wilbur Wright said no. Glenn Curtiss was dubious. But finally U.S. Navy Captain Washington Irving Chambers wrangled an enthusiastic exhibition flyer named Eugene B. Ely at a Maryland air meet.

The young civilian pilot was a Curtiss employee, with a secondhand pusher biplane that had been wrecked more than once. He flew in a stained leather jacket, with a pair of old motorcycle goggles and a battered football helmet for protection.

Ely seemed anxious to try the stunt to the point of recklessness. The Iowa-born flyer couldn't swim, was prone to seasickness, and was deathly afraid of the water. Perhaps equal parts patriot and showman, Ely swallowed his fears, determined to make the most of his chance at the dangerous pioneering flight.

His plane and its engine were hoisted onto the scout cruiser USS *Birmingham,* docked at Norfolk Navy Yard. The ship's crew had erected a sloping 83-foot platform on the vessel's forecastle to launch the fragile flying machine out over the water.

Ely and the Navy were in agreement that his chances were best if he took flight while the *Birmingham* was steaming in Chesapeake Bay. But while anchored, waiting for rain squalls to pass on the afternoon of November 14, 1910, Ely became anxious and gunned his engine, lurching forward early.

Agonizingly slow, his plane rolled down the ramp and dropped over the edge. Ely recovered from the plunge at the last possible second. His wheels had touched the dirty green water and the tips of his propeller splintered on the waves, but his plane chugged along, slowly climbing away from the murky brine that the flyer so feared.

On his first flight, Ely wore his football helmet, leather jacket, motoring goggles, and a lifejacket. He felt the latter impeded his movements of the plane's controls. In later flights, he abandoned the lifejacket and wore an inflated bicycle inner tube looped over his chest instead. (The Museum of Flight/Bowers Collection)

The first of countless takeoffs from a ship happened on November 14, 1910, when Eugene Ely's Curtiss Model D struggled off the makeshift deck of the cruiser Birmingham *in Chesapeake Bay. (The Museum of Flight/Hatfield Collection)*

Ely's Curtiss touches down on the deck of the Pennsylvania *in San Francisco Bay on January 18, 1911, jerking to a stop. The world's first arresting gear was made from 50-pound sandbags linked by lines stretched 12 inches above the deck. (The Museum of Flight/Bowers Collection)*

That evening, while Chambers congratulated the young pilot on his achievement, Ely told him, "I could land aboard too."

In early 1911, sailors built a similar platform over the stern of the armored cruiser USS *Pennsylvania* in San Francisco Bay for Ely's next demonstration. To halt the Curtiss pusher before it slammed into the vessel's superstructure, someone (no one remembers who for sure) came up with the idea of laying out ropes stretched between 50-pound sandbags on the landing deck. These would arrest the plane's forward motion before it smashed into the aft mast.

With hooks attached to the landing gear of his plane, Ely flew along the starboard side of the *Pennsylvania*, checking the platform, and then rounded the bow and flew aft along the port side. It was a landing pattern that would be mimicked millions of times by Naval aviators in the years to follow.

Behind the ship, the Curtiss bore in. Ely cut his engine while still poised over the water aft of the stern. As he came over the ramp, the air caught between the deck and his wings and bounced Ely's aeroplane higher, the outstretched ropes whizzing under the hooks. He dove for the deck, snaring the eleventh rope in the row and coming to a stop.

He had made it look easy. Considering the risks, dangers, and consequences of a single wrong move, it is a miracle that Eugene Ely didn't crash during one of these stunts. To call Ely lucky, though, would be misleading. Less than a year after the famous landing, he was killed in a crash during an exhibition in Macon, Georgia.

Luck had little to do with it. The pioneers of Naval aviation had simply chosen a difficult and dangerous profession. Most thought flying from a vessel was unnatural. Landing on the tossing deck of a ship was borderline suicidal. The fact that pilots might one day alight on the expansive deck of a huge flattop, at night, in a plane without propellers, seemed as impossible as flying to the moon. Many throughout the Navy establishment considered the whole matter of aviation a foolish, perilous pursuit.

In the years after World War I, most admirals were convinced that aviation had little to offer the fleet. Though flying machines had come of age during the battles in Europe, they likened the delicate biplanes to gnats – easily swatted away by ironclad cruisers or battleships. Aircraft were weak and frail. They couldn't fly very far and couldn't carry very much.

But there were some believers – a mutinous few in smoky back rooms who knew that the flying machine could, someday, really mean something. The place of these agitators in the Navy's pecking order could be derived from the choice for America's first, experimental aircraft carrier. The ship was slow and small, a retired coal-hauler named the USS *Jupiter* that had been destined for the scrapyard. Because the ship was electrically driven, it required a comparatively small crew, which was a main selling point to officials who otherwise saw the whole endeavor as "nonsense."

The ship was recommissioned as the USS *Langley* in 1922 – named after an airplane maker whose manned machines plunged into the cold water without a second of flying time. The new version of the old ship carried a relatively narrow wooden deck built from bow to stern, covering even the collier's weather-beaten bridge. The flight deck was supported by the vessel's former coaling masts, which had been chopped down to size. Soon after

her new life began, the ship was equipped with a pair of funnels that could be tilted down and away from the landing area during flight operations.

Early on it was clear that the *Langley* wasn't a true fighting ship. It was a slave to its aircraft and the winds. The ship was one of the slowest vessels in any armada. The "Covered Wagon," as flyers lovingly called the vessel, must have been an aggravation for fleet commanders. But the ship's value as an experimental test bed made the *Langley* worth its weight in gold to Navy pilots.

Many of the intrepid airmen who learned to fly from the *Langley's* decks went on to greatness as the carrier commanders of World War II. But in the 1920s, they endured what they dubbed "instrument panel face" – loose teeth, crushed noses, and black eyes from the violent and imperfect intersection of plane, aviator, and ship.

No one had yet created a true carrier aircraft, so pilots experimented with many different types of stiff-legged Navy machines on the *Langley's* tiny deck. A Vought VE-7 trainer flew from the *Langley* first on October 17, 1922. Days later, an Aeromarine 39 became the first to land on the converted carrier. Flyers in land-based biplanes, burly twin-engine machines, amphibious floatplanes, and even

The world's first true aircraft carrier was CV-1, the **Langley.** *Introduced in 1922, the vessel was a simple, slow-moving floating runway – nearly ideal for working out the basics of Naval flying. (The Museum of Flight/Bibbe Collection)*

With hooks affixed to its undercarriage, an Aeromarine 39B trainer flies over the deck of **Langley** *in late 1922. In the days before the historic first landing, LCdr. Godfrey de Courcelles Chevalier made innumerable practice runs. On October 26, 1922, the flyer eased the plane down, letting the wheels touch the deck and the hooks catch hold – making the first-ever carrier "trap." (The Museum of Flight)*

CLEAR THE DECK!

*In the water near the **Langley**, the pilot of a Vought VE-7 climbs from the cockpit of his smashed bird. After a failed landing, it appears that the plane hit the water, port wings first. Conveniently for the pilot, the Bluebird trainer appears to be floating nicely after the crash in 1923. (Naval Historical Center)*

an autogiro, all took a chance to brave the wind and the wires over America's first flight deck.

Sailors peeking over the edge of the deck witnessed spectacular sights as the aviators learned their new trade. Even a successful landing, some of them commented, was nothing more than a "controlled crash." And nearly every day, there were full-fledged crashes too – stalls, high bounces, and sickening slides. The ship's mechanics became expert repairmen, mending snapped struts, crushed wings, and a seemingly endless line of shattered wooden propellers.

As a machine was jerked to a halt by the primitive arresting wires or hit the rope crash barrier rigged beyond, the plane often upended. The *Langley's* teakwood deck soon looked like a butcher's block where countless propellers had bashed into its surface and shattered.

Despite the nearly constant carnage, fatalities on the flight deck were quite rare.

Even with the difficulties revealed by the *Langley's* operations, Navy commanders began to accept the value of carrying aircraft to sea. The design and construction of real, war-ready carriers was not far behind the small experimental ship.

Again, the Navy used hand-me-downs to create its carriers. The hulls of two partially completed heavy cruisers became the foundations for the great ships *Lexington* and *Saratoga*. The pair, commissioned in 1927, boasted improved sailing speed and much larger flight decks and aircraft capacity than the little *Langley*.

Aviators who had become used to the *Langley's* unimpeded flight deck scrutinized the *Lex* and *Sara's* expansive (and unforgivingly solid) island structure on

An NB-1 trainer assigned to *Langley* is hoisted out of the water after a bungled landing in 1925. The Boeing aircraft, one of 41 produced for the Navy, has seen its last day of flying. (National Archives)

This floatplane lost its ability to float immediately after an incredibly hard landing in the waters near Pensacola, Florida. The pilot escaped, but the passenger was killed. The accident took place in early 1937. The plane, though it's hard to tell for sure, was reported to be a Great Lakes TG-1. (National Archives)

CLEAR THE DECK!

*With its hook clasping a wire, a Loening OL-8 amphibian is photographed moments before touchdown on the deck of **Saratoga** in 1932. Early on, there was no such thing as a true carrier plane. All types of Navy craft, built for use on land and from the water, were flown from the carriers, too. (National Archives)*

*After flying from the open deck of **Langley**, Lexington's island structure, with gun turrets, smokestack, and massive bridge, looked like an awfully big hazard to carrier aviators. But, pilots said, at least the **Lex** had an expansive deck. Note the crash barriers and arresting wires arrayed aft of the open elevator. (The Museum of Flight/Bibbe Collection)*

the starboard side of the deck with some doubt. They predicted the island would create dangerous eddies and air currents over the deck. And, flyers knew, colliding with an 8-inch gun house or the massive smokestack on the right side of the "runway" was a real possibility upon landing, and perhaps, over time, inevitable.

But, they observed, at least the decks on the new ships were charitably wider and longer. Screw-ups would happen. There was little doubt about that. At least now there was a bit more room to attempt a recovery.

The new American carriers participated in many "fleet problems" during the 1930s, with Navy fleet commanders learning to use ship-based aircraft in mock fights for the Panama Canal, battles in the Caribbean, and, interestingly, carrier attacks on Pearl Harbor, Hawaii. The carriers and their aircraft were making inroads even with crusty old Navy types who still insisted that the battleship was king of the seas.

The "brown shoes" – Naval aviators – had already been won over. The *Sara* and *Lex's* ample decks and steady, sturdy hulls made landing safer and easier, trumping even the dangerous obstacle off the right wing. Sailors and flyers alike lovingly called the 33,000-ton vessels "boats."

Naval commanders, however, desired carriers that were smaller and lighter than the *Sara* and *Lex*. Bantam ships allowed for greater numbers of vessels to be built under a treaty that limited nations by warship tonnage. While many flyers privately groaned, the USS *Ranger* was commissioned in 1934. It was built for half the price of the

The rush is on to save this Great Lakes TG-2 as "Airedales" (carrier-deck crewmen) scramble up onto the high-side wing. The torpedo plane came to rest in the gun gallery of Saratoga *in 1932. (National Archives)*

big carriers, but the vessel was slow and lacked protection. Aviators complained that the ship's deck was small. The *Ranger* had bad elevators, no catapults, and inadequate ammunition storage. Many felt the Navy had made a $20 million white elephant on its first attempt to build a carrier from the keel up. Not equipped for the task, the *Ranger* never fought in the Pacific during World War II.

Beautiful new aircraft populate the cramped hangar deck of Ranger *in 1937. Hanging above is a Vought O3U-3 observation plane. Below is a Grumman J2F-1 Duck amphibious biplane. Space was at a premium on all carriers, but* Ranger *was smaller than most, making plane storage and handling problems especially acute. (National Archives)*

The battered hulk of a Vought O2U-2 Corsair serving with VS-2 is hoisted from the sea. The scout plane was most likely flying off Saratoga when it ran into trouble around 1931. A salvage effort for such a ravaged aircraft would never have been attempted during the war years. However, at the time, one sailor described the Navy as "miserly." (Naval Historical Center)

Strategists, tasked with anticipating threats, figured it would take at least six suitable combat carriers to fight the Japanese in the Pacific. The next two vessels, launched in 1936, helped America get closer to that goal. The *Enterprise* and *Yorktown* were judged by sailors and aviators to be good ships, "medium sized," with acceptable speed, modern plane-handling equipment, and adequate protection.

The new carriers brought the United States close to the quota permitted by international treaty. When the old *Langley* was reduced to seaplane tender status, it left the Navy about 15,000 tons with which to build. The *Wasp*, commissioned in 1940, displaced 14,700 tons.

Japan was a bit more lenient with its interpretation of the treaty. Monster carriers, bigger than the *Sara* or *Lex*, were passed off by Japanese officials as being 26,900 tons, missing the mark by as much as 11,000 tons. Eventually, leading up to the Japanese invasion of China, Japan's leaders announced their intention to ignore the agreement entirely.

The move inspired the United States Congress to authorize the construction of one additional vessel beyond the treaty's limits. The *Hornet* was similar to the *Enterprise* and *Yorktown* with slight improvements brought about by several years of evaluation. The *Hornet* began its service career on October 20, 1941, when it joined three other fleet carriers and the escort carrier *Long Island* in the Atlantic.

At the time, the Americans had three carriers operating in the Pacific: the *Lexington*, *Saratoga*, and *Enterprise*. The Empire of Japan had a fleet of six. At that moment, the Americans were out-manned, out-gunned, and under-equipped. The American vessels carried inferior aircraft, and U.S. Naval flyers were, to a man, "green" – still needing to prove their worth in battle.

Japanese leaders knew that the fortuitous gap between rival forces would not stay so wide for very long. If there was ever a time to strike, now was that time.

The Japanese viewed the U.S. Navy's small collection of carriers, along with a sizable armada of antiquated battleships, as the only force that stood between them and nearly total domination of the Pacific Ocean area. Conveniently, for the attackers, most of the American ships called a single port their home – Pearl Harbor.

After ditching on January 8, 1938, the pilot of this Vought SBU-1 scout bomber activated the plane's flotation bags. Now the waterlogged machine is being slowly towed to shore for salvage. Note the pair of wet flyers sitting in the boat. (Naval Historical Center)

Crewman make an attempt to recover a Vought SB2U-1 Vindicator that is dangerously close to tumbling over the side of the USS Charger during training exercises. If not for the main landing gear strut snagged in the vessel's gun tubs, the dive bomber and its two-man crew would have immediately plunged to the water below. (National Archives)

TOO LITTLE AND TOO LATE

For a moment in time, they were top of the line. But time had passed them by. The once modern, all-metal, monoplane fighting planes of the mid-1930s were "long in the tooth" by the outbreak of World War II – no longer able to defend themselves against skillful Japanese pilots and their agile planes.

When the Douglas TBD Devastator took to the air on its maiden flight on April 15, 1935, the big torpedo bomber was revolutionary. It was the first all-metal, low-wing monoplane to go into service with the U.S. Navy. It had a fully enclosed cockpit, hydraulically folding wings, and partly retractable landing gear. The plane's modern design and high performance for its day helped reinvigorate the art of aerial torpedo bombing, which had lost favor in the years before.

It could carry a half-ton torpedo affixed to its belly or 1,000 pounds of standard bombs. The first operational aircraft arrived for service with the Saratoga in late 1937

In its heyday, 1938, a shiny new Douglas TBD-1 Devastator torpedo bomber gets the signal to launch from Saratoga. The aircraft is from VT-3, with a torpedo-toting dragon painted on its side. Years later, VT-3 was assigned to Yorktown. This plane was most likely one of the many Devastators lost during the Battle of Midway. (National Archives)

and were well liked by flight crews. The Devastator was a rugged, dependable carrier aircraft and, in theory at least, a good warplane.

If the Americans had taken the Japanese a bit more seriously before Pearl Harbor, they might have been worried. Japanese aircraft were often dismissed as second-rate copies of western types – poorly armed and armored. However, the Nakajima B5N torpedo bomber, roughly contemporary to the Devastator, was significantly faster, could fly higher, and could carry more.

Comparing the Brewster F2A Buffalo against Japanese fighter types would have been another sobering experience. The Buffalo was another first for the U.S. Navy, an all-metal monoplane fighter with a powerful Wright Cyclone engine mounted in its barrel-shaped nose. When the first operational planes touched down on

Missing the arresting wires completely, this Devastator bounced over the side of Enterprise only to have its tail hook catch something solid at the last possible second on September 4, 1940. A sailor, leaning over the side, took this shot of the pilot and pair of crewmen scrambling to safety as their three-ton flying machine hangs vertically off the deck over the rolling waves below. (National Museum of Naval Aviation)

Pilots claim that some of the first Brewster Buffalos were spry little machines before they were loaded down with armor, self-sealing fuel tanks, radios, and the like. Here, a group of barrel-shaped F2A-2s shows off for the cameras near a stateside Navy base. (National Archives)

the deck of the Saratoga in 1939, it was considered a wonderful, spunky machine.

As salty Marine Corps ace "Pappy" Boyington so famously put it during one interview, "The early models, before they weighed it all down with armor plate, radios, and other shit, they were pretty sweet little ships. Not real fast, but [the Buffalos] could turn and roll in a phone booth."

For carrier operations, the Buffalo did have one frustrating quirk. When the little fighter landed hard (and nearly every carrier landing was somewhat rough), the plane's main landing gear strut would often buckle near the wing.

As time moved on, the Buffalo and Devastator were no longer "sweet little ships." At the dawn of World War II, they were liabilities. Though the Grumman Wildcat had lost out to the Buffalo in the 1936 fighter competition, the runner-up had now taken over as the preferred fighter for carrier duty. At the beginning of World War II, only a single combat-ready squadron of Marine Corps aviators still flew the Buffalo.

The Devastator was still out there, serving on the carriers, but it was due to be replaced by a new Grumman-designed torpedo plane. The TBDs proved incredibly vulnerable in combat and, sadly, the torpedoes they carried were often nearly useless. To maximize the

This Douglas TBD Devastator was yanked to a stop by the arresting wires just short of Yorktown's island structure, but a crooked approach left the torpedo bomber with its starboard gear over the side. Crewmen are beginning work to lift the plane back onto the deck. This accident took place on September 3, 1940. The plane was later shot down during the Battle of Midway. (National Museum of Naval Aviation)

chances of an effective run with their inferior weapons, Devastators had to come in slow and low, right into the teeth of the enemy's defenses. If the planes survived (which was a big "if"), they were left slowly clawing for altitude while fighting off attacks with their inadequate defensive armament.

At the Battle of Midway, both American planes came face to face with veteran pilots flying the potent Mitsubishi A6M Zero, with disastrous results. On the morning of June 4, 1942, the shore-based Buffalos of VMF-221 were scrambled to intercept a strike force of Japanese carrier aircraft headed for the island. The defenders launched 21 F2As into the skies, along with seven Grumman F4Fs. They dove into the

This pair of photos shows a Brewster F2A-3 Buffalo with one "foot" in the catwalk after a landing-gear failure aboard Long Island *near Palmyra Island in the Pacific. The machine belonged to VMF-211, a Marine flying unit that was the last front-line combat outfit to employ the Buffalo. These images were taken on July 25, 1942. (Naval Historical Center)*

massive formation of more than 100 approaching enemy planes, including droves of deft Zeros.

In the one-sided fight, 15 American pilots were killed. Two F2As returned to the airfield in flyable condition, with 13 shot down. In addition, two Wildcats were destroyed by the marauding Japanese aircraft. The Marines on the island began to call the portly Brewster fighters "Flying Coffins" and "Suicide Barrels." The plane would never see another minute of combat with the U.S. Navy or Marine Corps after that morning.

Brewster Aeronautical Corporation's advertising slogan was "For Mastery of the Air," but Marine Captain Philip White, a survivor of the savage air battle, bitterly expressed a much different opinion: "It is my belief that any commander who orders pilots out for combat in an F2A-3 should consider the pilot as lost before leaving the ground."

Hours later, TBDs from the American carriers approached the Japanese fleet in an uncoordinated attack and were also set upon by Zeros. Every Devastator from the Hornet was shot down. All but two Enterprise TBDs were destroyed. Four from the Yorktown, attacking in concert with Wildcat escorts, made it home. Out of 41 Douglas torpedo planes plodding along, slow and low, only six escaped the Japanese fighters and anti-aircraft.

Not one torpedo hit the enemy ships, and the once-advanced TBD was soon pulled from combat service.

Buffalos had a weakness in their landing gear that made many of them look like this after a rough carrier landing. On Long Island, men do their best to lighten the starboard side of the Marine Corps F2A-2 by adding their combined weight to the opposite wing in mid-1942. (National Archives)

CHAPTER TWO

CARRIER CLASH

In a real-world conflict between airpower and battleships, small planes launched from Japan's six aircraft carriers devastated the American fleet of old battle wagons at Pearl Harbor, Hawaii. Those who had long realized that Naval aviation would become a most powerful tool finally had their proof.

The December 7, 1941, Japanese assault left much of the U.S. Pacific Fleet in tatters, but no American carriers were in port that day. *Enterprise* and *Lexington* were delivering aircraft to Wake Island and Midway Atoll, respectively. And *Saratoga* was near California after completing an overhaul.

The absence of the American carriers was a stroke of luck that most certainly changed the outcome of the war. When the enemy's fleet carriers attacked, the old guard at Pearl Harbor took the blow completely. America's own

This F4F-4 Wildcat missed the wires and smashed into the cable barrier during flight operations in 1942. The plane's propeller has ripped through the carrier's deck, leaving gouges and loose chunks of wood. Note the fighter's unique fuselage-mounted main gear. Pilots say that the narrow-track gear, a design first used on aircraft with large center floats, made the fighter difficult to handle on crosswind taxies and during landings. (National Archives)

On a grass field in Bethpage, New York, a new Grumman TBF-1 Avenger is gingerly pulled back onto its gear after a hard stop tipped the big torpedo bomber up onto its nose. The plane is most likely one of the first made, with a paint scheme from the first months of 1942. (National Museum of Naval Aviation)

flattops, which would become so important in the years of fighting to follow, were off running errands on a Sunday morning.

More than a year before the fighting had started, a reporter asked Japanese Admiral Isoroku Yamamoto about his country's prospects, should there be a war in the Pacific. He responded, "In the first six to twelve months of a war with the United States and Great Britain I will run wild and win victory upon victory. But then, if the war continues after that, I have no expectation of success." U.S. and Japanese carrier forces clashed for the first time in month five of the conflict, in May 1942.

At this early stage in the fighting, America was on the defensive. Though the United States was outnumbered and, in many cases, outclassed by superior Japanese fighting ships and planes, American forces had one valuable advantage. Secret Japanese codes had been broken by cryptologists, allowing the U.S. Navy glimpses of the enemy's movements and strategies.

In early 1942, American cryptologists detected movement of Japanese ships and aircraft to Truk and Rabaul. Analysts correctly predicted that this meant an enemy thrust into the Coral Sea and, perhaps later, they mused, an attack on Midway.

The primary goal of Japan's Coral Sea foray was the invasion of Port Moresby in New Guinea. Capture of the city would allow the Japanese to control much of the Northern Australia and New Guinea areas and deny the Allies a potential air base within striking distance of the large Japanese naval base at Rabaul. The Japanese also desired a fight with the American carriers, hoping to force them into action, attack them, and send them to the bottom.

Seemingly fond of complex, convoluted strategies, Japanese commanders sent their forces into the area divided into multiple fleets, one of which contained two modern carriers, *Shokaku* and *Zuikaku*. The light carrier *Shoho* was assigned to escort the separate invasion task

A stream of fire-retardant foam arcs over the top of a Grumman F4F-4 Wildcat teetering on the deck of **Charger**. This crash took place on May 5, 1942. The aircraft was salvaged and returned to flying status, only to be more severely damaged in a landing accident more than a year later in Florida. The second time, the damaged plane was stricken from the Navy's records 16 days after the accident. (National Archives)

force. The Americans dispatched a fleet containing *Lexington* and *Yorktown* to the area to oppose the operation.

With both sides learning the new art and science of carrier warfare, each was nervous – and mistakes were made as the warships converged.

The Japanese attack planes found only an American oil tanker and its destroyer escort. With nothing else in sight, the flyers pounced on the hapless pair. The Americans were a bit luckier with their misdirected attack; while droning toward his target, an alert flyer from *Lexington* noticed the carrier *Shoho*, 30 miles to starboard.

Lexington and *Yorktown* Wildcat fighter escorts, Dauntless dive bombers, and Devastator torpedo planes closed in on the enemy light carrier. With only a few Zeros and outclassed Claude fighters airborne to stand in the way, U.S. Navy planes seemingly came from every direction, smothering *Shoho* with vicious aerial attacks.

Later in the war, Naval aviators learned to be more prudent, looking for new victims once their target was clearly incapacitated. But, during this first big carrier attack of the war, the *Shoho* absorbed 13 bomb strikes and seven torpedo blasts. The riddled vessel soon slipped beneath the waves. It was the first vessel larger than a destroyer lost by the Japanese during the war. Without the *Shoho* for protection, the balance of the enemy invasion fleet turned north, fleeing toward safer waters.

As evening approached, the Japanese had another stroke of bad luck. An attack group from their carrier force went out looking for *Yorktown* and *Lexington*. In the growing darkness and deteriorating weather, the planes jettisoned their bombs and torpedoes and turned back. They then stumbled onto the American fleet. Only a handful of the 27 Japanese planes survived the swarming Wildcats and the darkening skies to return home. Sailors noted that a few of the lost Japanese aircraft even

The remains of an F4F-3 Wildcat lost in training are photographed for the record. It appears that the Wildcat made a successful belly landing, but soon after, while still traveling fairly quickly, the fighter hit an embankment. The collision "knuckled under" the plane's Twin Wasp engine, ripping it from its upper mounts. The fighter is a total loss. (National Archives)

attempted to land on *Yorktown*, their pilots mistaking the American vessel for *Shokaku*.

By dawn on May 8, both fighting forces had finally located one another with scouting aircraft, and the real battle was about to begin. Almost simultaneously, each pair of carriers dispatched a strike force. The armadas of fighting planes, headed in opposite directions, passed one another in the skies over the Coral Sea. There was no time or spare fuel for a fight.

The carriers, of course, were the targets. The planes and pilots were of no consequence if they had nowhere to land at the end of the day's fight. In the ensuing exchange, *Lexington* and *Shokaku* were heavily damaged. *Yorktown* was hit by one bomb, but *Zuikaku*, hidden by clouds, was untouched by the American attackers.

The Battle of the Coral Sea was the first naval battle in history in which the fighting ships never came within sight of one another. All of the action was fought solely by aircraft.

TOUGH OLD BIRD

The Wildcat was so old that it had started life as a biplane. Conceived to replace the venerable Grumman F3F carrier fighter in 1935, the prototype XF4F-1 design was a two-winged affair, sticking to the Navy's proven formula of the time. But when the Navy signed a contract for the Brewster Buffalo monoplane fighter and more powerful engines became available, Grumman began to rethink its stub-nosed, dual-winged airplane.

The result was the Wildcat, the often outmatched but pugnacious Navy and Marine Corps fighter with a prominent cockpit, tubby fuselage, and plank-like wings. At places that the American public had never heard of before – Wake Island, Guadalcanal, and Midway – the Wildcat buzzed into the air to challenge veteran Japanese pilots and their outstanding aircraft.

Over Wake Island, the Marine fighter pilots bravely fought off aerial attacks and even sank a Japanese destroyer with their battered and often-patched Wildcats before they were forced to surrender. The men flew desperate missions until every one of their Wildcats was simply gone – bombed on the ground or blasted from the air.

Grumman ad men wrote, "It's just too bad for Tojo when one of our lads gets a bead on a Zero. American courage, American skill, plus a ship like the Wildcat is more than a match for the best the Jap has to offer!" At

Aboard Enterprise, *a barrel-nosed Grumman Wildcat attached to VF-6 gets the signal to launch. The plane is carrying a 100-pound bomb on its starboard wing rack. Note the second F4F-3 being readied to move into position as soon as the first has become airborne. (National Archives)*

CLEAR THE DECK!

best, it was stretching the truth more than a little bit. At worst, it was an out-and-out lie.

In a June 1942 combat report, LCdr. John Thatch said that the Wildcat was "pitifully inferior in climb, maneuverability, and speed" to the Japanese Zero. Together with other Navy pilots, the Arkansas flyer developed the "Thach Weave," in which two or more of the mediocre performing Wildcats could hold their own against the deadly Japanese fighter. Putting the Wildcat's armor and guns to good use, the two Navy pilots would weave, in a scissoring action, allowing one F4F to get a good shot at the enemy airplane trailing the other. When outmatched and alone, F4F Wildcats pilots often survived encounters by diving away at high speed – living to fight another day.

Though painfully aware of the plane's faults, pilots loved their Grumman fighters – primarily because they were tough. For example, Lt. Wilmer Rawie collided with a Japanese Claude fighter over the Marshall Islands in February 1942 and lived to tell the tale. The Claude's wing was smashed apart. But Rawie's Wildcat returned to the Enterprise with nothing but a missing antenna and a dent in its belly. The other pilots ribbed Rawie, claiming that he and his Wildcat were still dangerous, even if he had no ammunition.

The Wildcat was never as spry as the Zero, but it was better armed and well-armored – with self-sealing fuel tanks, armor plate, and a battery of four (and later six) .50-caliber guns.

Grumman, occupied with producing Hellcat fighters and Avenger torpedo bombers by 1943, transferred the job of building Wildcats over to General Motors' Eastern Aircraft Division. Eastern's FM-1 and improved FM-2 Wildcats saw extensive service on the Navy's escort carriers in the Atlantic and Pacific. The Wildcat fighters,

After what was penned at the top of the photo as "a freak accident," crewmen drag an overturned FM-2 Wildcat away from the bow of Makin Island. In order to right the aircraft, they must drag the three-ton fighter aft at least one plane length and then rotate the fuselage around the dead weight of its engine. (Naval Historical Center)

smaller than Hellcats or Corsairs, were a perfect fit on the space-pinched "baby flattops."

Wildcats flew missions until the end of the war – a testament to those at Grumman who started the project as a biplane 10 years before. And, in a time when the F4F was the best fighter the Navy had, pilots fell in love with the Wildcat. However, a few of the Naval aviators were still realistic enough to call their plane: "the ugliest frog-looking thing around."

This Cecil Field Grumman F4F Wildcat came down near Jacksonville, Florida, in 1942. While it looks like this had the potential to be a horrific accident, this fortunate flyer got away unscathed. The left wing absorbed the brunt of the blow, and the fighter neatly cracked open along the fuselage at station five, allowing the stunned pilot to simply unbuckle his harness and flop to the ground. (National Archives)

An FM-2 Wildcat, built by General Motors, makes a spectacular scene as it rips apart the flight deck. The fighter's landing gear has failed, yet the Cyclone engine and its propeller continue to roar. Moments after this image was captured, the plane and its shaken pilot bounced onto the deck and skidded to a stop. (National Museum of Naval Aviation)

Upon landing aboard Santee, the entire tail of this F4F-4 ripped free, sending (most of) the plane and pilot careening down the deck. The strange mishap took place during flight operations in the Atlantic in late 1942. When the fighter came to rest, its severed tail stood high in the air, the plane's propeller hub gouged into the deck. (National Museum of Naval Aviation)

The Navy offers all sorts of unique opportunities to those ready for adventure. But the pilot of this FM-2 probably wishes he could simply go home. Crewmen throw him a line as he begins his hair-raising escape from the cockpit, dangling about 40 feet over the waves. (National Museum of Naval Aviation)

A curious crewman leaned over the rail to shoot this image, downward, at a VC-68 aviator and his sinking bird after a failed landing aboard Fanshaw Bay. As the carrier steams by, the pilot lifts himself from the cockpit of his doomed FM-2. The fighter's nearly empty fuel tanks make it float well. (National Museum of Naval Aviation)

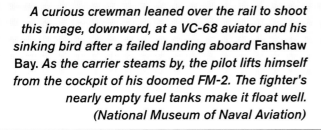

The Avenger was one of the most successful and valued aircraft in the Navy's inventory. The first TBF to arrive on Enterprise *made quite an impression, though maybe not a completely positive one. In this image, a large crowd gathers as men work to keep the big machine from pitching over the side. Note the brave deck crewmen who have climbed all the way up to the wingtip to most efficiently leverage their weight. This incident took place on July 23, 1942. (National Archives)*

As the fleets sailed away from one another, nursing their wounds, fires worsened aboard *Lexington*. The great ship was abandoned and sunk by a torpedo from a U.S. destroyer that evening.

Despite the loss of the *Lexington* (and an oil tanker and destroyer), many historians judge the Battle of the Coral Sea as a strategic victory for the Americans. The Port Moresby invasion force was turned back. The *Shoho* was sunk, and the Japanese naval air forces suffered significant losses. Heavy damage to *Shokaku* kept the carrier out of service for months.

One of the most significant results of the fighting in the Coral Sea was that neither *Shokaku* nor *Zuikaku* would participate in the next major naval clash. At Midway, three American carriers would face four Japanese flattops, instead of perhaps six.

Midway Atoll was located roughly in the center of the Pacific, about 2,800 miles from San Francisco and 2,200 miles from Tokyo. At the end of the Hawaiian chain, the small group of islands in the atoll held a remote American base some 1,300 miles northwest of Honolulu.

These images were taken of the sole survivor of a group of six Grumman TBF-1 Avengers detached from Hornet *to attack the Japanese carrier fleet from Midway. Ens. Albert Earnest brought the big torpedo bomber home riddled with holes. The tips of the propeller were bent when the right landing gear collapsed upon landing. The sheet, seen in the rear-view photograph, was most likely to cover the body of Seaman 1st Class Jay Manning, who was killed while operating the .50 caliber rear turret. The aircraft was later sent back to the United States for evaluation. (National Archives)*

Around June 24, 1942, this damaged and partly dismantled Wildcat was photographed on Midway's Sand Island. The plane was flown by VMF-221 pilot Capt. John Carey, who was wounded in action while defending Midway from attack on June 4. Note the rudder, which used to carry red and white horizontal stripes. Weeks before the battle, the rudder was painted over with a more subdued blue. At the same time, the red circles in the center of the national insignia were also covered in order to avoid confusion with the Japanese national insignia. (Naval Historical Center)

Japanese commanders viewed Midway as part of the Empire's defensive perimeter in the northeast Pacific. Offensively, if Midway could be taken from the Americans, it left the Hawaiian Islands vulnerable to attack.

Midway was also psychologically important to the United States. The last thin line of American defense between Hawaii and the enemy, the tiny scrap of sand and coral was something the United States had to fight for. The Japanese viewed the outpost as a perfect trap to lure the American carriers into a fight and use their superior naval forces to the greatest advantage.

Once the United States' Navy was ineffective in the Pacific, the Japanese would be virtually unopposed. As Yamamoto had predicted, for at least six months he would "run wild," scoring victory after victory against the Allies. On June 3, 1942, Americans had been fighting Japan in the Pacific for just a few days shy of that six-month mark. That day, an American patrol plane discovered an approaching invasion fleet of Japanese warships and transports 500 miles from Midway, closing in fast.

True to form, the coming attack was multi-faceted and complex. There were the invasion fleet of transports and escorts (which had just been spotted), a separate group of four carriers, an armada of heavily gunned battleships, a line of submarines to be used as sentries, and a diversion force (including two additional carriers) to the north.

What followed the initial sighting of the invasion force was failure after failure of American airpower, with one marvelous exception.

Land-based Army B-17s rumbled out to the Japanese vessels first and dropped payloads from high altitude. Their bombs missed the ships, sending up only splashes of water. Navy patrol bombers were next, attacking the group that night. They fared only slightly better. A single torpedo from the attacking PBY flying boats hit the bow of a Japanese oiler, but it kept going, along with the rest of the fleet.

The next morning, aircraft from the four Japanese carriers, *Kaga*, *Hiryu*, *Akagi*, and *Soryu*, launched a strike on Midway's ground facilities. Marine F4F Wildcats and outmoded F2A Buffalos scrambled to intercept, but they could do little but fight to save themselves from the Zeros and their veteran pilots. Midway's buildings and hangars were blasted in the attack, though few men on the island were killed, and the runways remained operational.

A group of four Army B-26 medium bombers and six land-based TBF Avengers, loaded with torpedoes, went looking for the Japanese carriers that morning. When they found the enemy vessels, the attackers were severely mauled by Zeros on combat air patrol.

The only Avenger to survive the attack took off from Midway with pilot Ens. Albert Earnest at the controls, gunner Seaman 1st Class Jay Manning assigned to the upper turret, and young Radioman 3rd Class Harry Ferrier in the plane's belly.

When the formation of bombers found the Japanese carriers, they moved in close to release their torpedoes. As Manning readied his .50 caliber gun, he called out Zeros diving to intercept. Meanwhile, Ferrier, stationed at the tunnel gun at the bottom of the plane, could not see any of the Japanese fighters as they bore in. Frantically scanning his assigned portion of the sky, he heard

Warrant Machinist Tom Cheek of Yorktown *shot down three Zeros during the attacks on the Japanese carriers at Midway. Returning to the ship with a damaged tail hook, his F4F-4 hit the barrier hard and flipped. Cheek opened his seat belt and scrambled free of the wreck. The battered fighter was photographed, still overturned, on a dolly on the carrier's hangar deck. (National Archives)*

This Dauntless dueled with Japanese gunners aboard the Kaga *on June 4, 1942. The SBD-3 came home, but the enemy carrier did not. Here, the dive bomber, assigned to VB-6 on* Enterprise, *is pictured on the deck of* Hornet. *Pilot Ens. George H. Goldsmith and Radioman 1st Class James W. Patterson, Jr. were forced to land their shot-up machine on the nearest available flight deck when their fuel ran low on their way home. (Naval Historical Center)*

A battle-damaged Dauntless skids into the water alongside an American cruiser during the Battle of Midway. A number of difficulties could lead a pilot to choose a landing at sea instead of trying for a carrier deck. Hydraulic failure, damage to landing gear, a blasted tail hook, or lack of fuel were some of the most common problems. The flyers in this SBD experienced the latter. The ship is the heavy cruiser Astoria. *It carries a Curtiss SOC Seagull scout plane on its amidships catapult. (Naval Historical Center)*

Manning firing his gun at the enemy fighters and then felt the thump of bullets cracking through the hide of the torpedo bomber.

Manning's gun fell silent as the Avenger dove toward the water. Ferrier looked up over his shoulder to see his crewmate hanging lifeless in his harness – there was no doubt Manning had been killed.

More Zeros appeared and made their firing runs. In a dreamlike state, Ferrier recalls catching a glimpse of spent Japanese bullets rattling around in the bottom of the Avenger's fuselage as more holes appeared, letting in daylight. The helpless radioman dutifully stuck to his assigned position – the lower gun – until hydraulic fluid sloshed over the viewport and the bomber's tail wheel popped down, blocking the muzzle.

A moment later, a whizzing bullet hit Ferrier in the wrist and another nicked his forehead, knocking him unconscious.

The pilot of the bomber wasn't doing much better. Ens. Earnest grimly flew on toward his target. He received a gash in the neck from flying shrapnel as the brutal attacks continued.

With severed elevator controls and dying hydraulics, Earnest feared he was losing control of his aircraft as the plane dove toward the sea. The pilot kicked the rudder, slewing the TBF to the side to launch its torpedo at a nearby light cruiser. Just 30 feet above the sea, Earnest was able to roll the elevator trim tab back far enough to arrest the crippled plane's dive before it hit the water.

Then it was a race for cover as the Zeros continued to make passes at the lone American survivor of the ill-fated attack. Suddenly, Earnest was alone in the sky. He was alone in the airplane too – Manning was dead and Ferrier was lying unconscious. Though the plane was sieved with more than 70 holes, it was still flying. He turned east, toward home. All of his navigational instruments were smashed, hanging from the ragged instrument panel. It didn't matter. Soon enough, he spotted the black smoke curling up from Midway.

Out of the 10 aircraft that were dispatched to duel with the Japanese fleet, only Earnest's maimed Avenger and two B-26 bombers made it back. The Japanese carriers easily dodged the slow-moving "tin fish" they delivered. Some of the torpedoes were even spotted and machine-gunned in the water as they slowly plodded toward the Japanese warships.

Aircraft from *Yorktown*, *Enterprise*, and *Hornet* were next to attempt an attack, hoping to catch the enemy carriers as they recovered aircraft from their strike on Midway. Disorganized, many of the American Douglas TBD torpedo planes arrived first with no fighter cover for protection. At low level, the combat air patrol Zeros went to work on the slow blue bombers, decimating the machines as they jockeyed to launch their second-class torpedoes from a suitable distance. Nearly all of the planes were destroyed.

However, the terrible sacrifice of the Naval aviators and their low-flying TBDs greatly influenced the battle. The Zeros were drawn low to prey on the nearly helpless machines, leaving the skies above relatively clear when

Following their safe return on June 4, 1942, Douglas SBD-3 Dauntless pilot Ens. Jim Riner, Jr. and his gunner, Floyd Kilmer, discuss the anti-aircraft damage they collected during their bomb run over a Japanese carrier near Midway. The aviators were members of Hornet's VB-8. *(National Museum of Naval Aviation)*

the American dive bombers arrived on the scene at higher altitudes.

The Japanese carriers were caught with aircraft and weaponry all over their flight decks. The protecting Japanese fighters struggled to reach the plummeting Dauntless bombers and their Wildcat escorts. Three bombs smashed into the *Akagi*, setting off terrible fires as torpedoes, bombs, and fueled aircraft burned furiously. The attack on the *Soryu* was similar. American flyers bore in to deliver three solid hits, creating towering, violent flames. The *Kaga* was hit by four plummeting bombs from the SBDs, including one that detonated on the carrier's bridge. Again, secondary fires and explosion raged.

Meanwhile, unaware of the results of the battle, deck crewmen aboard the American carriers went through the gamut of emotions. The torpedo bombers' expected return time came and went. The sky, for the most part, was devoid of aircraft. It was soon clear that they had been slaughtered.

Next, the Dauntless dive bombers and Wildcats filled the landing pattern. After their fight, some of the planes were blasted and holed. A few came in with no hook or one wheel jammed. As they thumped down on the deck, aviators jumped out of their cockpits. Elated, they excitedly recounted their successful attacks and the furiously burning enemy carriers they had left behind. The sailors hung on every word.

Only the *Hiryu*, some distance from the others, escaped the American's only successful air attack in so many costly attempts. The remaining Japanese carrier launched a pair of strikes, aimed at evening the score with the Americans.

Both waves of aircraft found *Yorktown*. The Japanese aircraft waded through fighter protection and anti-aircraft fire to deliver their weapons. *Yorktown* was heavily damaged by three bomb strikes and two torpedo hits. Though still afloat, *Yorktown* was unable to recover its aircraft, and her planes landed on other American carriers.

That evening, *Enterprise* and *Hornet* SBDs (along with a few refugees from *Yorktown*) found *Hiryu* and ravaged the last Japanese carrier in the fight. The U.S. victory was nearly absolute. The enemy invasion force turned back, and four of Japan's six valuable fleet carriers were lost.

The *Yorktown* was lost, too. The ship survived the attacks and was being towed back to Pearl Harbor when Japanese submarine *I-168* torpedoed the wounded carrier and an escorting destroyer, *Hammann* (DD-412), sinking both.

The Battle of Midway was the turning point in the Pacific war. Japanese carrier strength was severely limited by the losses. Not only were the four carriers destroyed, but many of the enemy's best naval aircraft and most skilled pilots were gone, too. The balance of power had begun its shift to the side of the Americans.

After Midway, aircraft from Japanese and U.S. carriers clashed twice more in 1942, in the waters near Guadalcanal in the Solomon Islands. While both nations lost ships, aircraft, and fighting men in the protracted struggle on and near the island, only the United States had the ability to recover from the losses relatively quickly. Yamamoto's promised months of victory had come and gone. Japan was now on the defensive.

THE TURKEY

Pilots said that the name "Grumman" on an airplane was as good as the word "Sterling" on silver. And so it was with Grumman's replacement for the aging TBD torpedo bomber. Naval flyers initially considered the big, boxy machine a "scaled-up" version of the Wildcat fighter – high praise in their book. The new plane turned out to be every bit as tough and reliable as Grumman's famous fighter plane.

First flown on August 1, 1941, the prototype Grumman TBF was rolled out of the Bethpage, New York, factory for public viewing on a cold winter day, December 7, 1941. The news of Japan's attack on Pearl Harbor prompted Grumman officials to name their new aircraft the "Avenger."

Interestingly, at Midway, the Avenger's combat debut went nearly as badly as it did for the outdated Douglas Devastators it was slated to replace. Unescorted, six TBF Avengers detached from the USS Hornet took off from Midway Island looking for the Japanese carriers. They found them. And as the burly Grumman aircraft rumbled in to deliver their "tin fish," Zeros appeared, intent on repelling the attack. Only one of the new torpedo bombers made it home, crash landing on Midway with one flyer dead and the others wounded. The machine was sieved with bullet holes.

Even though its opening battle ended in a grim defeat, the Avenger was soon recognized as a useful and potent combat aircraft, finding its way onto nearly every carrier in the U.S. fleet and Britain's Fleet Air Arm. The plane was certainly better than the Devastator in almost every way. The new machine was faster, more powerful, able to carry more payload, and better equipped to defend itself against hostile fighters.

The well-liked bomber was truck-like when it came to maneuverability, but rock steady for delivering explosives – the job it was designed and built for. Pilots said the plane was easy and honest, giving "the comforting impression of vicelessness."

Rocket-armed Avengers from the escort carrier Tulagi rumble over Iwo Jima on March 2, 1945. The TBMs were tasked to fly attack missions against the island's fortifications. The bombers were also used on long anti-submarine patrols to protect the American ships involved in the invasion from surprise attack. (National Archives)

Deck crewman began to good-naturedly call the plane "The Turkey." On final approach, moments before landing, the Avenger certainly did look like an ungainly bird, with its nose in the air, big wings wobbling from side to side, and its gangly main gear hanging below.

When Grumman became overloaded with successful aircraft projects needed for the war effort, Eastern Aircraft, a division of General Motors, began making Avengers. Nearly identical to the Grumman TBF aircraft, the license-built Avengers were designated TBMs. Both companies combined built a total of 9,836 of the strikingly large, heavy, and capable combat machines.

The death of much of the Japanese navy helped push the Avenger beyond the torpedo bomber role in the last years of the war. Hunting for submarines or pounding island strongholds like Iwo Jima and Okinawa, TBMs often left their torpedoes behind, hefting depth charges, aerial rockets, or conventional bombs instead.

Avenger pilots adopted a shallow-glide bombing approach, which often exposed them to more enemy fire than the plummeting dive bombers or swifter fighters. As a result, many of the machines came home blasted by ground fire. Amazing photographs were taken of Avengers missing seemingly vital components such as an entire horizontal stabilizer or a sickeningly large portion of one wing. But the planes came back, limping to the carrier on a prayer, and on Grumman's exceptional workmanship.

Used to patrol for submarines during the war, the dependable and versatile Avenger was retained in the U.S. fleet and acquired by other nations in peacetime. TBMs re-equipped with special sensors and radar became anti-submarine warfare aircraft, serving into the 1950s. One of the countries that operated the Avenger after the war had seen the plane in action many times before. A handful of the planes, best known in their heyday for fighting the Japanese, were acquired by the Japanese maritime self-defense force.

Though sprayed with holes in a Japanese artillery attack on an airfield at Bougainville, this Marine Avenger was up flying combat missions the next day. Corporal Joseph Vedova of Cleveland, Ohio, and his crew worked throughout the night of March 8, 1944, to fix the sieved bomber's nearly 400 shrapnel punctures. (National Archives)

Showing the ungainly configuration that inspired crewmen to call the Avenger "The Turkey," an injured torpedo bomber approaches the carrier Essex. The VT-83 machine appears to be coming in a touch high for its one-wheeled attempt, though the LSO (on the right) seems to find the approach acceptable for the TBM-3's imminent crash landing. (National Museum of Naval Aviation)

Avengers sometimes carried a string of twelve 100-pound bombs to blast craters in Japanese island airfields. This TBM-3 from Suwanee returned with one of the explosives still in its bomb bay, overlooked by the radioman on May 24, 1945. The bomb bay window had been sprayed with hydraulic fluid when enemy gunfire hit the plane over the target. Upon landing, the bomb slid forward and exploded, killing the pilot instantly and injuring 13. Another aviator in the plane later died from his injuries. (National Archives)

An Avenger plunges into the water off the port side of a carrier after dragging its wing across the deck. The bomber was most likely caught in a torque roll following a wave-off, the pilot adding power to its big Wright R-2600 Cyclone radial engine too quickly to get out of a jam. Now, as some pilots were fond of saying, he and his crew are "going swimming." (National Archives)

All over the flight deck and the island of the Chenango, crewmen cringe and cower as a TBM-3 makes a hairy landing on March 17, 1945. Will the wire pull the plane to a stop before the starboard wing smashes into the escort carrier's island? The men nearby do not seem anxious to stand around and find out. (National Museum of Naval Aviation)

SLOW BUT DEADLY

Some claimed that the Douglas SBD was an outdated machine by the time war came to the Pacific. The first version of the dive bomber was a Northrop design, making its maiden flight in 1938. But after the fighting started, it seemed that when good things happened for the Americans, they came on the wings of the venerable machine named Dauntless.

At the Battle of the Coral Sea, 13 bombs delivered by SBDs smashed into the deck of the Japanese carrier Shoho, sealing her fate and causing one dive bomber commander to excitedly radio the American fleet, "Scratch one flattop!"

When used in desperation to keep Japanese planes away from the U.S. carriers, the lightly armed dive bombers were swarmed by Zeros. SBD pilot Stanley "Swede" Vejtasa found himself cornered by eight of the Japanese fighters. Turning into his attackers, he told his gunner, "Keep your head and conserve ammunition." In the epic 40-minute fight, Vejtasa shot down three of the aggressors and escaped to fly again. So skillful at air fighting, the young lieutenant was quickly transferred to fighter duty.

At Midway, the SBD fought on. The Douglas machine turned out to be worth its weight in gold when its pilots sunk four Japanese aircraft carriers. The blows delivered by Dauntless aviators won the critical engagement – in a battle that many say turned the tide of the war in the Pacific.

Flyers loved their plane, even if it was an aged design plodding along at a lethargic pace. SBD stood for "Scout

A group of SBDs from VB-10 cruise over Palau on March 30, 1944. The aircraft were assigned to Enterprise. Note the gunner in the rear of the Dauntless, at the ready with his twin .30-calibers. (National Museum of Naval Aviation)

Bomber, Douglas," but flyers joked that it was "Slow But Deadly."

Pilots noted that the machine was tough, too. It had to be to survive the high stresses of an all-out dive under fire. One reporter went along for a ride and described his plummet. "We fought blacking out. We had the feeling we were being pulled through knotholes. Wind screamed past us. The earth rushing up at us.

"Then came the pullout, the moment when a dive bomber hits bottom. Suddenly every tiny bit of workmanship that went into it becomes vital. Our SBD bucked and rumbled. The stress was unbelievable," he reported. The pilot took the dive he'd done hundreds of times before much more casually, calmly reassuring, "It's a sturdy ship. It'll take a lot and won't mind a bit."

Over North Africa, a Dauntless caught a German tank out in the open and strafed it with its dual forward-firing .50-caliber nose guns. The low-flying pilot was a bit too anxious, though, and plowed through a stand of trees. Douglas used the incident in its advertising, reliving the moment that the battered SBD returned safely, skidding to a stop on a carrier. The ad shows the mangled plane, with bent prop, ripped cowling, and chewed-up wings, while the deck crewmen look on in awe.

When Curtiss SB2C Helldivers began to replace the old SBDs in late 1943, many flyers were heartbroken by the change. The new machine was faster, more powerful, and could carry more, but the Dauntless was a pilot's plane. As Time magazine put it, "She had no bugs, no streaks of temperament; she was a thoroughly honest aircraft. She could take a frightful beating and stagger home on wings that sometimes looked like nutmeg graters."

On March 18, 1943, this Douglas SBD-4 hit the rail of the control tower and smashed into the ground at the Marine Corps Air Station in Mojave, California. The flat-hatting pilot was taken to the hospital with "multiple, extreme injuries." Incredibly, the mechanic riding as a passenger walked away with only minor cuts and bruises. (National Archives)

SLOW BUT DEADLY CONTINUED

After nine months of combat service, a bleached and battered SBD-3 Dauntless was returned to California. The wreck, formerly operated by VMSB-132, was deposited at the Douglas Company's El Segundo plant in February 1943. There, those who had worked to build the aircraft could see how their handiwork had held up after exposure to the harsh combat conditions of the Pacific. (National Museum of Naval Aviation)

The pilot of an SBD-2B Dauntless prepares to climb down from his nosed-over dive bomber as deck crewmen look on. Observers report that the crash was caused by "holding off" (failing to promptly push forward on the stick) after the cut sign was given by the LSO. The result was a stall, flattened left wing, and a mangled propeller. The accident happened during training aboard Charger on September 10, 1943. (National Archives)

This SBD-5 hit the crash barrier arrayed across the deck of Lexington. The violent collision cracked the engine mounts, collapsed the port gear, twisted the propeller, and smashed the wingtip – most probably a total loss. Note that the VB-16 Dauntless has fake gun ports painted into the leading edges of its wings. (National Museum of Naval Aviation)

With other aircraft in the pattern, a Douglas SBD gets a bit of assistance in vacating the landing area. The carrier deck crane was often nicknamed "Tillie the Toiler" by crewmen – a name that was taken from a character in a newspaper comic strip. The dive bomber appears to have nosed over upon landing, perhaps collapsing its port landing gear. (National Archives)

CHAPTER THREE

NEW BLOOD

The opposing fleets had worn each other out by the close of 1942. As 1943 dawned in the Pacific, there were no epic carrier versus carrier battles like those seen in the months before. Many of both nations' flattops were on the bottom.

The Japanese navy was smarting from the loss of *Shoho* at the Coral Sea, four fleet carriers at Midway, and *Ryujo*, which *Saratoga's* planes sunk near Guadalcanal on August 24, 1942. Japan scrambled to convert other vessels into carriers, affixing flight decks onto the hulls of seaplane and submarine tenders and passenger liners.

Beyond the vanquished ships, the once-proud Japanese navy required time to replace squadrons of aircraft and legions of first-rate flyers lost at sea. Many

American pilots noted that, after Midway, the air-fighting skill of the average Japanese naval pilot was never again the same.

America was even worse off when it came to carriers. *Lexington*, *Yorktown*, *Wasp*, and *Hornet* were gone, leaving only the *Enterprise* and *Saratoga* in the Pacific. And there were tense times when one of the surviving pair was laid up with repairs or overhaul, leaving a lone carrier at sea.

After the heavily damaged *Hornet* sank on October 27, 1942, *Enterprise* was the only American carrier available in the Pacific, leading the crew to display a banner that read: "*Enterprise* vs. Japan." When the "Big E" was pulled away for overhaul, *Saratoga* was joined briefly in the Pacific by HMS *Victorious* – the British carrier "on loan" through

The wing of this F4F-4 from VC-11 slammed into the 40mm anti-aircraft gun mount at the bow of the escort carrier Altamaha *during a botched takeoff in 1943. The Wildcat plunged into the water and the pilot was soon picked up, unharmed, by the plane guard destroyer. (National Museum of Naval Aviation)*

This F4U-1 Corsair rests 10 miles north of Eastland, in north central Texas in early 1943. The gear is down and locked, and the engine appears to have been running when the plane came down into this rough terrain. Note that the tail hook looks as if it was deployed at the time of the accident. (National Archives)

after months of vicious air, land, and sea fighting. Victory at the small jungle outpost allowed for aircraft to operate from Henderson Field and made it possible for subsequent attacks upward (northwest) on the Solomon chain.

American forces took New Georgia, Vella Lavella, and Bougainville, driving out the Japanese and setting up airfields as they went. Each jump of this first leg of the island-hopping campaign brought the powerful Japanese naval base at Rabaul a little bit closer.

The Japanese navy was still quite dangerous, but Allied forces were making inroads to contain the mighty fleet. The Japanese needed carriers, planes, and men, all of which were slow in coming from the small, resource-starved islands of the Empire. For the United States, the outlook was much brighter.

In 1943, a jaw-dropping transformation took place in the number of resources available to the U.S. Navy. Not counting the *Essex*, which officially entered the Navy's roles on the last day of 1942, 15 large aircraft carriers were commissioned in the calendar year of 1943. U.S. shipyards also launched the hulls of 41 small escort carriers, which would serve with Great Britain and the United States in both the Pacific and Atlantic. Never again would the Americans be nervously holding the line with a lone carrier in the massive Pacific.

New aircraft, in great numbers, also started to arrive in the fleet. Grumman Avenger torpedo bombers, which

America's leanest time. The *Saratoga* and its British counterpart sometimes swapped aircraft as they operated near the Solomon Islands.

Even though carriers were nearly an extinct breed, the war rolled on. American officials declared Guadalcanal in the southern Solomon Islands secure on February 9, 1943,

After an abrupt stop in the crash barrier, a TBF-1 Avenger settles back onto its gear aboard the Block Island *in April 1943. The propeller is wrecked, and almost certainly the Wright Cyclone engine is, too. The plane is assigned to VC-25, which flew from the carrier off California during its shakedown cruise. (National Museum of Naval Aviation)*

debuted at Midway, arrived to displace the battered and nearly worthless Douglas Devastators on carrier decks.

And though the first Vought Corsairs weren't ready for carrier use, Marine pilots took possession of the fighters, flying from islands in the South Pacific. The first such land-based Marine units flew from Henderson Field on Guadalcanal starting on February 11, 1943.

To the jubilation of many haggard Wildcat pilots, new Grumman F6F Hellcat fighters began to arrive on the decks of the new carriers. Aviators thought of the new fighter as the "Wildcat's big brother" – appreciably faster, bigger, and more powerful. If they liked the Wildcat, they loved the Hellcat.

Just as the United States was able to outdistance the Japanese in the construction of fighting vessels, so it was

with aircraft, too. During the war years, the Japanese Empire was able to build about 74,600 new fighting aircraft. In the same span of time, 299,000 warplanes (of all types for all branches in all theaters of war) winged away from the seemingly always-operating U.S. aircraft factories.

There were new flyers coming, too. In 1941, the U.S. Navy trained 3,112 new pilots, up from 708 the year before. In 1942, the first full year of war, 10,869 men earned their wings of gold. In 1943, the number jumped to 20,842.

It was more than a question of quantity. Starting with *Essex*, commissioned December 31, 1942, America's big new carriers were some of the most advanced and resilient in the world. The vessels had an improved elevator arrangement that helped make aviation operations safer and faster. Unencumbered by pre-war international

A few days in May 1943 saw the men on the deck of Independence doing a lot of manual labor. Wildcat fighters, which seemed to refuse to stay on their landing gear, were manhandled around the deck. The top image shows an F4F being shoved onto the elevator on May 1. Two days later, another fighter came to grief and had to be quickly pushed forward. (National Archives)

THE PUSSYCAT

Grumman's F6F was the old cat with new tricks. The fighter was touted as a bigger and better version of the F4F Wildcat, and the Hellcat was instantly popular with pilots. While they liked the fact that it was faster and more powerful, flyers were fond of the Hellcat's small improvements, too – it had guns that were charged by switches instead of the cumbersome pull-handles of the Wildcat. And no longer would airmen have to crank the landing gear up by hand after takeoff; in the Hellcat, it was as simple as flipping a lever.

The XF6F-3, one of the Hellcat prototypes, ran into trouble on August 17, 1942, when its R-2800 engine quit over Long Island, New York. Pilot Bob Hall glided the new plane down into a farmer's field for a wheels-up belly landing, severely battering the Grumman fighter. But the Navy recognized the Hellcat as an outstanding aircraft design, and the orders continued.

Another Hellcat's engine died on a delivery flight near Cape May, New Jersey, in January 1943. Navy pilot Casey Childers dead-sticked the heavy machine into a stand of pine trees. Though the F6F disintegrated into a tumbling mess, observers were stunned to see that the shaken flyer emerged unharmed. The new Hellcat, a product from Grumman's "Iron Works," was just as tough as the Wildcat had been.

When Grumman began work on a new building to hold Hellcat production, the company purchased recycled steel from New York City's elevated railway. And aviators soon joked that the steel girders from the "Second Avenue El" were used in the making of the hearty Hellcats themselves, not the factory.

Indeed, some of the most prolific flyers in the fleet touted the F6F's toughness in battle. Leading Navy ace David McCampbell wrote, "The Hellcat was a source of continual amazement for me. One of our planes accumulated 117 bullet holes and still made it back to the carrier. I was shot up by anti-aircraft fire over Marcus Island to the extent of a belly tank being on fire, a hydraulic fluid fire in the fuselage, loss of rudder control, loss of hydraulic power for lowering the wheels, complete loss of radio, yet I was able to make it back to my carrier 135 miles away."

Aboard Yorktown, a Hellcat pilot jockeys his fighter into position for takeoff. The F6F was assigned to VF-1, the "High Hatters." This photo was taken in June of 1944. (National Archives)

After its engine seized, one of the prototype Hellcats ended up in the middle of a Long Island farm. Some said the plane skidded to a stop in a potato field, while others recalled working amid string beans. The mechanics who were sent out to retrieve the plane didn't really care. The XF6F-3 carried a new R-2800 that conked out at high speed during test flight number five. Test pilot Bob Hall guided the stricken machine down to its bumpy belly landing on August 17, 1942. (Northrop Grumman)

Besides the F6F's signature stoutness, other traits made it superior to the Japanese Zero. The Hellcat was speedier by around 50 miles per hour and had better armor and heavier armament. With all of the weight in guns, protection, and a big engine, the Hellcat was naturally able to dive away from a Zero, but not climb or maneuver with the same swiftness as the Japanese fighter.

Another comparison one can't help but make when considering the Hellcat is how the plane stood up to its brother carrier fighter, the F4U Corsair. The latter was faster, more maneuverable, and more versatile, but it was also more difficult to master. Pilots found that the Corsair was high-strung and temperamental. On the other hand, the F6F was "nothing but a big ol' pussycat," said airmen – "big, tough, and honest." One aviator was reported to have exclaimed, "If this Hellcat could cook, I'd marry it!"

The one thing that can be said for sure is that the Hellcat was the workhorse of the war in the

The torque of the Hellcat's engine at full throttle made the plane want to turn left on takeoff. This pilot seems to have set his rudder trim tab a bit too much to the right to counteract the effect. His F6F-3 leaves Hornet at a dangerously crooked angle during the launch of a strike on Formosa. (National Archives)

THE PUSSYCAT *CONTINUED*

Pacific. The Grumman F6F destroyed a stunning 5,156 enemy planes in the air, around 75 percent of all Navy aerial kills. For every Hellcat lost in a dogfight, the F6F shot down 19 adversaries.

Despite the fighter's command performance in the biggest theater of the greatest war in history, the Hellcat was phased out of Navy front-line service soon afterwards. While Corsairs were still in the fleet during the Korean War, the faithful and steady F6F fighters were deemed expendable. Some were converted to drones and loaded with explosives to intentionally crash, "kamikaze-style," into Korean strongholds.

When the arresting wires jerked this Hellcat to a stop aboard **Ticonderoga**, *the plane's fuel tank kept going. The auxiliary tank was chopped open by the propeller and exploded. As flames consume the left side of the fighter, the pilot prudently rolls out of his cockpit on the right side. (National Museum of Naval Aviation)*

CLEAR THE DECK!

With a broken back from a bone-jarring landing, this Hellcat is towed forward on the rainy deck of Essex. The Hellcat was judged incredibly tough, but there was a limit. Designers had to balance the strength-versus-weight equation, coming up with a compromise. When an aviator came in too fast or too high, the airframe simply couldn't take the stress. (U.S. Navy via Paul Madden)

This flyer from Lexington missed the wires and flipped during a landing aboard Belleau Wood on August 30, 1944. "Asbestos Joe" (right) was on the scene in seconds to pull the pilot free. However, the aviator died from head injuries. Deck crewmen on the carrier speculated that the pilot neglected to snug up his harness, and it may have cost him his life. (National Museum of Naval Aviation)

After a gear collapse, crewmen work to put the wheels down on a wrecked fighter aboard Yorktown *in May 1943. The starboard wing of the Hellcat has been badly crunched in the accident. The crewmen, working fast, have brought up a dolly to roll the wounded fighter away if they fail in their attempts to get the gear down quickly. (National Archives)*

(SBDs or SB2Cs), and 18 torpedo planes (TBFs).

Just days after the *Essex* officially came into being at Newport News, Virginia, the Navy commissioned another carrier in Camden, New Jersey. Like its big brother, the *Independence* was also the first in a long line of similar vessels destined for battle in the Pacific. Compared to the *Essex* ships, the *Independence* class of light carriers were not as universally well liked.

When it became apparent that the carrier was the new capital ship, designers created the *Independence* light carriers from converted cruiser hulls. The first ship in the series began its existence as the hull of the future light cruiser *Amsterdam* before being switched. The light carriers were less stable and slower than the big fleet carriers and set sail with narrower, shorter flight decks. Pilots were quick to note that it was much easier to get into trouble on the often-pitching, always-narrow deck of a light carrier.

The ships initially went to

treaties, the *Essex* class ships had long and wide flight decks and hangar decks, and they were able to launch more aircraft into battle at a faster pace. Defensively, the heavy ships carried improved armor, anti-aircraft guns, a superior system of compartments within the hull, and the latest search radar.

The carrier crews nicknamed the force of aircraft launched by the *Essex* class as "Sunday Punch." The air group consisted of 36 fighters (F6Fs), 36 dive bombers

sea with nine fighters, nine dive bombers, and nine torpedo planes. The complement of aircraft was adjusted to 24 fighters and nine torpedo planes when it was found that the dive bombers required more deck length than was available to take off safely when heavily loaded with bombs.

Incredibly, over the year of 1943, the United States commissioned an *Essex* class carrier about every 52 days. An *Independence* class vessel joined the fleet roughly every 40 days.

Wires dig into a wayward FM-1 Wildcat on the deck of Block Island *in May 1943. In seconds, the forward motion gone, the fighter will fall back down on its wheels. The escort carrier was off California, on its way to the Atlantic to hunt submarines. The ill-fated vessel was torpedoed and sank off the Canary Islands a year later. (National Museum of Naval Aviation)*

The new ships ushered in the next phase of the Pacific war, as America went on the offensive. The new carriers often worked in strong, mobile groups, their aircraft focusing on attacking shore installations instead of Japanese vessels.

As well as supporting Army and Marine landings on islands such as Tarawa and Makin Atoll, the planes in the new, fast carrier task forces could appear, seemingly from nowhere, to harass nearby Japanese forces, particularly air bases. This diminished the enemy's ability to respond to an invasion once it was underway.

The new tactics took precision, timing, and practice. To the joy of the "old salts" who had held the line with a depleted fleet, the new ships, aircraft, and commanders were finally arriving on the scene. Leaders viewed an attack on isolated Marcus Island as "practice" for the great raids to come.

August 31, 1943, saw the *Essex*, the *Independence*, and the new *Yorktown* appear within striking range of Marcus. The island was too remote for invasion. Commanders simply ordered their pilots to do as much damage as possible, leaving Marcus a backwater wreck in the greater

Though the Navy often vigorously defends its ownership of crashed aircraft, this SBD-4 looks like it will forever belong to no one but the swamp. The Dauntless, from Naval Air Station Dayton Beach, Florida, was photographed on May 20, 1943. Though it was just days after the crash, the bomber looks as if it has been resting there for months. (National Archives)

drive to Japan's homeland. The mass of warplanes launched from 130 miles out, and appeared at the tail of a towering thunderstorm that hid them until the last moment.

Bearing down on the fat, triangle-shaped island, the fighter pilots were perhaps more antsy than usual, ready for their first taste of battle in the Grumman Hellcat fighter. When no enemy aircraft came up to protect the installation, they dove in to "beat up" anything they could find with their six machine guns – including planes on the airfield, anti-aircraft gun emplacements, and ships anchored nearby.

Blasts and smoke from Japanese guns, black from 3-inch guns and white from 20mm and 40mm bursts, appeared around the planes as they briskly went about their work, riddling Betty bombers with bullets and igniting fuel trucks and ammunition dumps.

The SBDs plummeted down from above, delivering 1,000-pound bombs. Some of the TBFs arrived in shallow dives, dropping 2,000-pound "blockbusters" onto the runways, hangars, and buildings nearby. Later estimates

The men stationed at Daytona Beach use a truck-mounted crane to retrieve the remains of a Douglas SBD-4. The crash looks to have been the result of an engine failure. As the carcass is lifted high, men work to steady the bomber as the wrecker moves over the bridge. The crash took place on June 19, 1943. (National Archives)

For the aviators aboard, this is one of those times where fractions of a second must seem like hours. While they clutch the canopy rail, they ponder: Will the old girl flip all the way over or thump back down, blue side up? This image of a teetering Dauntless SBD-4 was taken aboard Independence during the ship's shakedown cruise in 1943. The plane was assigned to VC-22. (National Museum of Naval Aviation)

Wheels don't roll so well when oriented this way. This Hellcat's strut failed during a landing aboard Cowpens on July 3, 1943. The strut and wheel were designed to rotate 90 degrees (in the opposite direction) so the wheel would tuck in flat inside the wing when the landing gear was up. (National Archives)

This doesn't look like it will turn out too well. Judging by the crewmen in the background, who are beginning to scatter, they don't think so either. With its tail hook clattering along the port catwalk of the Cabot, this TBM-1 Avenger looks as if it will miss the wires entirely. The VT-31 torpedo bomber came to grief on December 14, 1943. (National Museum of Naval Aviation)

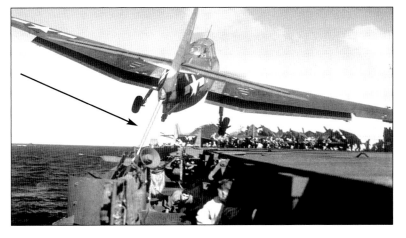

ESCORT CARRIERS IN THE ATLANTIC

In the first years of the war, German U-boats preyed heavily on Allied ships traveling between the United States and Britain. From late 1939 though 1942, millions of tons of valuable fuel, food, and equipment settled to the icy bottom of the North Atlantic after successful attacks by enemy submarines.

The U-boats did the most damage in an area known as the "air gap" in the middle of the Atlantic Ocean, south of Greenland. Here, hundreds of miles of open sea were out of reach of even the longest-range Allied patrol bombers. American sailors called the hunting grounds "Torpedo Junction."

March 1943 was a new low for the merchantmen, with 108 vessels sunk as wolf packs again stepped up their attacks in the North Atlantic. But it was the last days of what the German U-boat men called "happy times." New technologies, improved tactics, and hard lessons learned allowed the Allies to fight back effectively against the sea hunters.

The USS Bogue, a small escort carrier, began its duties crossing the Atlantic that month, and more of the "baby flattops" soon followed. The vessels carried up to 24 aircraft – Wildcat fighters and Avenger bombers. The planes worked to close the air gap, swooping down on any U-boat seen in the vicinity of the plodding supply ships.

As more new escort carriers steamed from U.S. shipyards and were assigned to the Atlantic, the vessels' roles switched from that of defensive tool to offensive weapon. Teaming up with destroyers, each carrier formed the nucleus of a "hunter-killer" team – actively pursuing U-boats, cornering the warships, and sending them to the bottom.

A TBF-1 Avenger went almost totally off the deck before its tail wedged into some machinery on the side of Card in mid-1943. The escort carrier was training in Chesapeake Bay at the time of the accident. The bomber was assigned to VC-1. Now crewmen must devise a way to coax the heavy plane back onto the deck. (National Museum of Naval Aviation)

Radar or sonar found the quarry, and the destroyers and Navy planes piled in. If the submarine dove under the waves, the destroyers attempted to force it back to the surface with depth charges. Once up, the planes, painted gull gray and insignia white to blend in with the often-stormy skies, ferociously attacked the trapped U-boat.

A hunter-killer aviator's delight was to encounter a "milch cow" submarine in the midst of re-supplying a depleted U-boat at sea. The Wildcat fighters usually came first, blasting away to subdue the vessel's anti-aircraft gunners. Then the slower Avengers came in with a heavier punch in the form of depth bombs and rockets.

Also in the Avenger's arsenal was a secret anti-sub homing torpedo, appropriately nicknamed "Fido." Once dropped, the slow-moving torpedo would circle at a depth of 50 feet until its hydrophones picked up the sound of its prey. The weapon would then close the distance with its electric motor. Once near its target, Fido's 92-pound warhead exploded.

Cautious handling and a protective screen of destroyers usually kept the hunting escort carrier from becoming the hunted. The small carriers were notoriously light, with thin armor. Sailors joked that the only way an escort carrier would get hit by **two** torpedoes was if the second one hit the truck light on the top of the mast as the sinking ship plunged beneath the waves. They were wrong. When a U-boat crept within range of the USS Block Island, it took three torpedoes to sink the baby carrier. It was the only escort carrier lost in the Atlantic. The German submarine crew paid for the victory with their lives when U.S. warships pounced on the attacker and sent it to the bottom.

The flyers from the first escort carrier to serve in the North Atlantic racked up the most impressive record. Though it was sometimes difficult to confirm submarine "kills," sources state that the Bogue's aircraft, along with her escorts, sank 12 or 13 enemy submarines between May 1943 and April 1945. In total, hunter-killer teams dispatched approximately 35 U-boats, and forced the Germans to withdraw their once-successful wolf packs from the Atlantic.

Lots of manpower is put to good use to save this Avenger aboard **Bogue** on June 19, 1944. The crews are trying to lighten the load on the gear stuck on the catwalk and yank the big machine sideways. The TBM is equipped with 3.5-inch aerial rockets, used in hitting U-boats. (National Archives)

In high seas, Solomons loses a pair of Wildcats during a particularly severe roll on July 31, 1944. The Avenger in the center of the image also looks like it has partly broken loose. Deck crewmen rush in to arrest the dangerous situation on the pitching deck. (National Archives)

When this TBF-1 struck the ramp of the escort carrier Solomons *on March 25, 1944, it looked as if no one would survive the horrific collision and fire. The VC-9 aircraft, equipped with rockets, was brought in too low and slow. The pilot painted himself into a corner. Two of the flyers involved in this wreck were pulled from the sea alive after their smashed Avenger slipped into the water. Their luck was short lived – the pair were killed a month later when their new aircraft crashed during an attack on a German U-boat. (National Museum of Naval Aviation)*

When this TBM ditched, it hit hard. The Avenger's wings were bent backward from the collision with the water. As the heavy engine begins to take the plane down, only one of the three flyers has freed himself from the aircraft. (National Museum of Naval Aviation)

Everyone onboard Bunker Hill *watches as Tom Blackburn's F4U-1 Corsair overturns in the barrier in July 1943. Though it was an exceptional fighter, qualifying the Corsair for carrier service proved to be a daunting task. Difficulties with the plane's landing gear, aerodynamic characteristics, and visibility delayed its integration into the fleet for more than a year. (National Museum of Naval Aviation)*

revealed that roughly 70 percent of the Japanese hardware on Marcus Island was destroyed by the marauding flyers after several attacks during that day.

The mission was considered a success. It was not only the first combat use of the Hellcat, but also the debut of the two new types of U.S. carriers. The damage to the installation came at the cost of three fighters and a single Avenger, all from *Yorktown.* They were all lost due to heavy Japanese anti-aircraft fire.

Several more aircraft came back with holes and other damage. After a plane caught the arresting wires and taxied forward, the pilot would give a "thumbs down" signal to a plane inspector if his aircraft were a "dud" – damaged in the fight or with some component not functioning properly.

The inspector, upon examination, could also "down" the aircraft. Crewmen attached a yellow or red flag to the machine's radio antenna mast. Yellow was used to indicate minor repairs that could happen on the flight deck. Red meant the plane would go below to the hangar deck for more serious work. In this way, the number of

Marine pilot Lt. Donald Balch contemplates his good fortune. He lived to fight another day after his F4U-1 was riddled by Japanese fighters over New Georgia. The VMF-221 pilot coaxed his blasted Corsair home to the Russell Islands on July 6, 1943. (National Museum of Naval Aviation)

the largest American task force of carriers yet seen in the Pacific, consisting of six flattops.

As preparation for the invasion of the Gilbert Islands commenced, Navy carrier aircraft ranged far and wide in an attempt to eliminate any Japanese air threat that might hinder the landings. The airfield on Mili Atoll in the Marshall Islands received a visit from marauding American Naval aircraft on November 16, 1943.

Charles Crommelin, the flight commander of the *Yorktown's* aircraft, was badly hit when a Japanese shell exploded near the cockpit of his speeding Hellcat during the attack. Instinctively, he yanked up on the stick and the fighter obeyed, clawing up to 3,000 feet.

"Arky" Snowden loses the tail of his F6F-3 while landing aboard Belleau Wood *in August 1943. The front two-thirds of the fighter scooted between the ship's stacks and dropped to the water. Only the plane's tail and right landing gear stayed on the deck. A destroyer picked up the pilot just as the ripped-apart Hellcat slipped under the waves. (National Museum of Naval Aviation)*

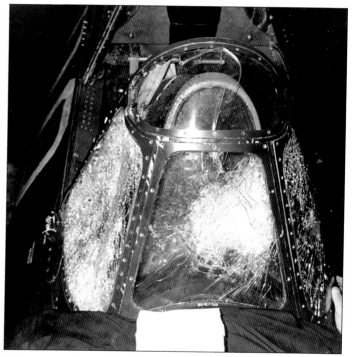

This image shows the shattered windscreen of Charles Crommelin's Hellcat, "00." He flew the plane back to the Yorktown *partly blinded by flying glass and severely injured. Once evacuated to Pearl Harbor, Crommelin is rumored to have limped into the officer's club for a belt of Old Fashioned, still wrapped like a mummy in bandages. "I didn't want a drink," he explained later, "I just wanted to show those kids it's not too tough to get shot up." (National Archives)*

aircraft down for repairs, and conversely, the number of planes on the deck that were ready to fly, could be reported to the air officer, captain, and commanding admiral almost immediately after a strike mission.

Weeks later, three other recently arrived carriers, the new *Lexington*, *Princeton*, and *Belleau Wood*, hit the Gilbert Islands on September 18. Then, the ever-growing U.S. fleet viciously walloped Wake Island on October 5 and 6. It was

vas hit badly. Crommelin knew it right away. The
is finger was gone, his wrist was most likely
broken, and a jagged piece of metal protruded from his
leg. Worst of all, the blast had "frosted" the canopy with
a web of cracks and sprayed Crommelin with thousands
of shards of glass. He could only see from one eye. There
was blood everywhere.

He looked for his wingman, sliding back his canopy
with his wounded hand. Tim Tyler, a relatively new pilot,
had eased his fighter close beside Crommelin's. He looked
over at his flight leader, wide-eyed. Crommelin managed
a half-hearted wave.

Then his engine started to fade. The injured flyer
pawed for the choke handle and pulled it toward his
bloody flight suit. The engine coughed and roared back
to life. But as soon as he let go of the knob, the choke
snapped back toward the shattered instrument panel and
the engine again wound down.

With the control stick between his knees and one
hand holding the knob, Crommelin gingerly groped
around the cockpit floor with his bleeding hand. He
found a pencil, broke it in half, and stuffed the pieces
under the knob. The Hellcat's engine began to purr
again.

*The pure muscle of Lexington's deck crew drags a
wounded Hellcat out of the landing area during flight
operations on December 6, 1943. It can't be easy to budge
the five-ton fighter with its left wing dragging and a flat
tire. However, the smashed plane has to move – more
fuel-starved aircraft are in the landing pattern.
(National Archives)*

*Alongside Belleau Wood, an
Avenger from VT-1 comes to rest
after a textbook ditching
attempt. All three crewmen can
be seen leaving the TBM-1 –
near the cockpit, turret, and in
the water beyond the tail. This
action took place on September
2, 1943. (National Archives)*

Maybe he'd make it back to the *Yorktown* after all, he thought. He would have to do some pretty fancy flying to get aboard with one eye and hardly any forward visibility. He really had no choice. Odds were he wouldn't survive ditching next to a destroyer.

It was mostly up to Tyler, who guided him 120 miles to the ship and into the *Yorktown's* landing pattern. Seeing his beloved "boat" was enough to make Crommelin grin, but the cold air pounding into the cockpit stung his teeth. They had been chipped by flying glass.

Crommelin's gear, flaps, and hook came down normally. He uttered a quiet thanks to the men and women at Grumman's "Iron Works" for creating such a durable airplane. Crommelin squinted towards his wingman's Hellcat, flying in tight formation off to one side of his fighter.

When the LSO gave the "cut" sign, Tyler relayed the order through hand signals as he "poured on the coals," climbing away. Crommelin's battered F6F snagged a landing wire and lurched to a stop. He had to be lifted from the cockpit. The doctors were amazed he'd made it – they found he had collected more than 200 wounds

from the exploding shell. Pilots on *Yorktown* were astounded, too. To them, it seemed, the pilot and the plane should have gone down soon after they'd been hit.

An SBD-5 drops into the water off the deck of Cabot on October 1, 1943. This action took place when the carrier was fairly new, preparing for battle in the Pacific by training in the Chesapeake Bay. The aircraft was assigned to VC-31. (National Museum of Naval Aviation)

An F6F-3 skids off the deck of Barnes on October 22, 1943. The pilot attempted to regain flying speed after getting the cut signal. The Hellcat smashed along the catwalk, killing a 20mm gun crewman, and then went over the side. The pilot, Ens. Olinyock, sank with the plane. (Naval Historical Center)

This amazing series of photos shows an accident that took place on the deck of the escort carrier Barnes on October 24, 1943. When Ens. Schroeder's F6F-3 landed short, his hook became hopelessly bent in the landing lights on the aft edge of the ramp. Traveling over all of the wires without catching any of them, his fighter crashed through the first barrier and somersaulted while tangled in the second, flipping the aircraft down the elevator shaft. The elevator was lowering another Hellcat, manned by Ens. Boyd Weber. No one was hurt in the crash. (National Archives and National Museum of Naval Aviation)

This famous image shows an F6F-3 Hellcat half into the Enterprise's catwalk on November 10, 1943. The pilot received a wave-off signal during landing. As he began to pull away, his fighter dragged its left wing, caught a wire, and settled onto the ship at a crooked angle. As the flames spread, catapult officer Lt. Walter Chewing, Jr. bravely climbed up the side of the fighter to help the pilot get out. The VF-2 flyer, Ens. Byron Johnson, escaped without serious injury. (Naval Historical Center)

Turned back with a gas leak, Lt. Alfred Magee, Jr.'s Hellcat began to trail fire before his emergency landing aboard Cowpens. Once the plane came to a halt, Magee rushed off the right wing and firefighters pounced on the blaze. The fire was out in a minute and a half. The tense moments took place on November 24, 1943, during attacks on the Gilbert Islands. (National Museum of Naval Aviation)

CHAPTER FOUR

THE TURKEY SHOOT

America and its ever-growing carrier force voraciously ate up the miles to the Japanese homeland in steady bites, each island outpost receiving unannounced visits from seemingly relentless swarms of angry blue Navy planes.

Following the occupation of Tarawa in late 1943, the Marshall Islands became the next Japanese base on the target list. The invasion of Kwajalein Atoll on January 31, 1944, signified the first breech of Japan's "Greater East Asia Co-Prosperity Sphere."

A savage attack on the enemy naval base at Truk in the Caroline Islands and the occupation of Eniwetok

followed in February. Landings at Hollandia in northern New Guinea came in April. Both sides prepared for a summer that would bring about bitter fighting for the Marianas and parts of the Caroline Islands.

At a slower rate than the Americans, the Japanese were struggling to replace the flattops, aircraft, and experienced pilots lost in clashes at Coral Sea, Midway, and in later battles. Shortages of fuel and the threat of prowling American submarines had largely kept the Japanese navy on the defensive throughout 1943.

In a role reversal from the early months of fighting, the Americans now worked to devise a plan to draw the remaining Japanese carriers into a final fight, hopefully eliminating them from the scene for good. The initial attacks and landings on Saipan in the Mariana Islands finally brought out

The tail of this SB2C-1, assigned to VB-15, was chomped by another aircraft aboard Yorktown on January 2, 1944. The plane was parked forward when a landing plane jumped the barrier, stopping only after ripping into the rear of another Helldiver. (National Museum of Naval Aviation)

The American flattops readied a strike force to hammer Guam's airfields when more pressing matters intervened. Radar showed large numbers of aircraft moving in from the west – it was a wave of aircraft from the long-awaited Japanese carriers.

The U.S. launched some 450 aircraft from 15 fleet and light carriers at the 70 Japanese attackers. The enemy planes that somehow managed to avoid the swarming Hellcats encountered a wall of anti-aircraft fire from American ships. In return for the massive Japanese loss of equipment and men, only a single bomb lightly damaged the battleship *South Dakota*.

A second wave was spotted on radar at a distance of 115 miles, an hour after the first. The 109 Japanese fighters and bombers had only slightly more luck than the others, causing a handful of casualties on carriers *Wasp* and *Bunker Hill*. But this second wave of attackers was ravaged as well.

Japanese commanders kept feeding valuable fighting men and planes "into the fire," so to speak, launching a third and fourth wave of aircraft, many of which could not locate the American fleets. However, the Grumman fighters spotted many of the planes as they headed in to land at airfields on Guam and Rota. More nearly irreplaceable Japanese men and machines fell to the American pilots, who were not above kicking the Japanese when they were down.

After the war, officials estimated that out of the 326 aircraft launched by the Japanese that morning, 220 of them were shot down in what Naval flyers would call the "Great Marianas Turkey Shoot." Japanese woes were compounded when American submarines torpedoed the carriers *Taiho* and *Shokaku*.

the enemy carriers in force and led to the final great air and sea battle of the war.

As bombing and shelling attacks on the island began on June 13, 1944, the U.S. submarine *Redfin* spotted a large fleet of Japanese warships and carriers underway near the Philippines. It would be days before they arrived in the battle area. The invasion of Saipan commenced on June 15.

Stationed to support the amphibious assault, the American fleet cautiously eyed the sea and sky, awaiting the inevitable arrival of the enemy's carrier forces. While the Americans focused most of their attention west, the first threats to the carriers came from land-based aircraft from Guam on the morning of June 19. Combat air patrol Hellcats defended the U.S. fleet without trouble, and more American fighters followed the enemy to its source, fighting over Guam with some 35 Zero fighters.

HOSE NOSE

Chance Vought's design V-166B was a winner, but the plane's fate was suddenly in jeopardy when a company pilot got lost in bad weather, ran low on fuel, and decided to put the prototype Corsair down on a golf course fairway near Norwich, Connecticut.

As if he was thumping down on the deck of a carrier, Boone Guyton hit the rain-soaked grass with a three-point landing and immediately began to slide. With a crunch – sickening to a pilot and heart-breaking to a designer – the beautiful silver machine flipped and twisted, finally jerking to a stop against a large stump.

It was a miracle that the pilot was not seriously hurt. It was even more of a miracle when the plane was dragged out of the rough and revived in Vought's factory. The rebuilt long and lanky aircraft with the powerhouse engine and distinctive inverted gull wings nudged past the vaunted 400 mile-per-hour mark just a few months later, in October 1940.

The F4U Corsair and the Hellcat were the big, powerful, and fast Navy fighters that helped turn the tide in the Pacific – able to defeat the once-dominant Japanese Zero. But it is there that the similarities end. Pilots said that the Hellcat was a big, lovable lunk – almost easy to fly. The Corsair was often more troublesome, tricky, and dangerous, particularly in the final stages of a carrier landing.

While the Corsair was even better than the Hellcat in many respects, the machine that was a dream in the air was a nightmare operating from the "no-room-for-error" deck of an aircraft carrier. The pilot, sitting well behind the plane's wings, had a hard time seeing where he was going. They jokingly called the Corsair "Hose Nose" and "The Hog."

At low landing speeds, the Corsair had the nasty habit of stalling out, one wing before the other. And, perhaps worst of all, the fighter bounced high on its stiff main landing gear oleos, often missing the arresting wires completely. And, after missing the wires, nothing good ever happened. As a macabre

Over time, the Corsair was assimilated into carrier duty. These F4U-1Ds were assigned to VMF-114 and flew from Essex in July 1944. The Corsair today on display in the Smithsonian's Udvar-Hazy Center near Dulles Airport carries the colors and markings of the fighter in the foreground, the "Sun Setter." (U.S. Navy via Paul Madden)

joke, some flyers called the Corsair "The Ensign Eliminator."

While the troubled but promising F4U was kept off U.S. Navy aircraft carriers for many months, the Marines had no such worries. They took the plane to operate from airfields on islands throughout the Pacific – where the Corsair's good traits were warmly welcomed and the plane's carrier woes nullified.

Many Marine squadrons, including Gregory "Pappy" Boyington's famous VMF-214 "Black Sheep," flew the F4U from godforsaken island outposts more than five times as often as they ever would from carriers during the war.

One Marine even used the trusty F4U itself as a weapon when needed. Robert Klingman was on the tail of a high-flying Japanese Nick fighter when he found his guns had frozen. Slowly gaining on his target, he guided the whirling propeller of his Corsair into the tail and rear cockpit of the enemy plane. The Nick plunged into the sea, and Klingman, his dying Corsair sputtering in protest, coaxed his fighter-turned-buzz-saw back to an Okinawa airfield.

After a long delay and many adjustments, the Corsair came to the carriers too, joining the Hellcat to batter the dying Japanese air forces. With many of the enemy's best pilots gone and their aircraft in short supply, the F4U was also drafted into operating as an attack plane, equipped with bombs, rockets, and napalm. Japanese soldiers on Iwo Jima and Okinawa learned to dread the peculiar whistling sound made as air howled through the intakes on the wing roots of a diving Corsair.

After the war, the Corsair was judged better than the Hellcat and, amazingly, the planes continued to be produced. The venerable planes participated in the Korean War, often in the role of fighter-bomber. The last Corsair rolled off the assembly lines in early 1953, a version destined to serve with the French navy.

A Corsair that hit the barrier and flipped up on its nose is gently lowered back onto its gear aboard Essex. Note the wires, chocks, and front group of men, all holding the fighter in place as the men in back draw the tail back down. One crewman is already up on the wing, removing the fighter's ammunition. (U.S. Navy via Paul Madden)

With other aircraft stacking up in the landing pattern and no time to spare, a "pranged" F4U-1D is winched, pushed, skidded, and lugged forward, as is, to clear the deck of the *Windham Bay*. The image was taken from the escort carrier's island on May 2, 1945. (U.S. Navy via Peter Bowers)

This F4U-1D veered off the runway and demolished a twin-engine Beech JRB at Marpi Point on the island of Saipan. Front-line fighter planes were built to be much stronger than non-combatant–type utility aircraft: while the Beech has been hopelessly chopped apart, the Corsair is relatively intact. The collision occurred on July 20, 1945. (U.S. Navy via Peter Bowers)

The pilot must have been shocked to still be alive when he unbuckled his harness and stepped out of this wreck. It used to be an F4U-1A Corsair, assigned to VMF-913 at Cherry Point, North Carolina. Aviators have said, "When it looks like you're going to crash, try and keep flying the biggest piece." Lieutenant W.E. Mattram's "biggest piece" had no control stick, instrument panel, or engine when it finally slid to a stop in mid-1945. (U.S. Marine Corps via Dick Rainforth)

Marine Lt. Bob Klingman used his VMF-312 Corsair as a buzz saw by ripping into the rear end of a Japanese Nick reconnaissance plane after his guns had frozen. Safely back at Okinawa, the aggressive Marine pilot was photographed with the damaged tips of his fighter's propeller. The strange victory took place on May 10, 1945. (National Archives)

A Goodyear-built FG-1D Corsair bounced along a marshy area after overrunning the runway at Cherry Point, North Carolina. However, the big plane had nowhere near enough momentum to carry it over the creek. The wing-folding mechanism may have broken on impact or, more likely, the wing was lifted by crews beginning the recovery efforts. The accident took place in 1945. (U.S. Marine Corps via Peter Bowers)

This has trouble written all over it. Shooting upwards, a lensman in the starboard catwalk of the escort carrier Natoma Bay *captures the form of an FM-1 Wildcat flying where it doesn't belong. The fighter's left horizontal stabilizer caught on the escort carrier's web of wires and antenna, twisting the plane sideways and depositing it in the water. The accident took place near Majuro Atoll on February 7, 1944. (National Museum of Naval Aviation)*

Late on the afternoon of June 20, American search planes found the remaining Japanese carriers nearly out of range to the west. Admiral Marc Mitscher had only minutes to decide. An attack would be risky. The aircraft would return low on fuel and have to land at night. However, if the remaining enemy carriers could be caught and sunk, it might forever bring an end to the threat of the Japanese fleet. Gambling the lives of his flyers, he decided to try.

It was 4:21 PM when the carriers turned into the wind to launch aircraft. It would be dark by 6:40 PM Still, 216 aircraft rumbled into the air, each pilot and crewman hoping that this sunset wouldn't be his last.

The American planes reached the Japanese fleet at a distance that made everyone wonder if any of them would make it back. Quickly, they dove in to deliver their bombs and torpedoes while the fighters spread out to give cover.

After a rush job, perhaps 20 minutes of fighting, the planes hurriedly headed east in small groups. Their actions had not decimated the Japanese fleet as Mitscher had hoped. But the raid did lead to the destruction of the

carrier *Ryujo,* along with a pair of oilers. The *Zuikaku,* the only surviving carrier to participate in the Pearl Harbor attack, was severely damaged by a bomb. Other ships in the armada, including three light carriers, suffered minor damage.

The Navy pilots were most concerned about making it home as the light faded behind them. Even with their carriers steaming to meet them, the agonizing race between rapidly disappearing fuel and the slowly passing miles was going to be too close to call.

There were some who knew they weren't going to make it. Many Curtiss SB2C Helldiver pilots stared at their gauges in the waning light and knew they were going swimming later in the evening. The flyers, most of whom liked the old Douglas SBD better, cursed their heavy, big-tailed monsters.

It was 10:45 PM before the fuel-starved aircraft found the carriers. The scene was a mess – desperate flyers chasing the wakes of blacked-out ships in the pitch dark of night. The air crackled with the sound of pilots reporting battle damage, positions, and, most of all, their

What's left of this Vought F4U-1 lies, absolutely mangled, on O'Hare Field on Apamana Island in the Gilbert Islands. The VMF-422 fighter was destroyed on February 28, 1944. Just a month before, the snake-bitten Marine fighter squadron lost all but one of its aircraft and six pilots when they flew into a massive storm. It is unclear whether this Corsair was the sole survivor of that ill-fated flight or a replacement aircraft. (National Archives)

When this SBD-5 of VB-10 was hit over Palau on March 30, 1944, it developed a massive oil leak. Here, another flyer pulls in close to get a photo of the blackened machine as it struggles to the Enterprise. To save weight, the rear guns have been tossed overboard. Because he was unable to see through the oil-soaked windscreen, the pilot chose to ditch the wounded plane at sea. Both men were rescued. (National Museum of Naval Aviation)

universally desperate fuel status. Planes began to flop down in the water amid the ships, their bone-dry tanks keeping them afloat for several minutes while the flyers climbed into their rafts.

Mitscher was compelled to do the unthinkable; he ordered the fleet to turn on its lights. The action was a calculated gamble on the part of the admiral to save his airmen. Mitscher was once a carrier flyer himself. And while many historians note that the order to light up the fleet made the ships "sitting ducks" for enemy submarines, the decision was perhaps less risky than his choice to launch his evening attack.

THE LANDING

An aircraft carrier was always a dangerous place. But pilots said nothing was more demanding and hair-raising, than a carrier landing. The task of aircraft recovery took fine-tuned cooperation, timing, precision, and more than a little skill. There were about 30 different things that could happen as a heavy, high-performance war machine

*An LSO aboard the **Essex** mimics the attitude of an approaching Hellcat in mirror image. This landing took place in January 1945. Note the plane guard destroyer trailing behind the carrier, should a flyer and his plane go into the water. (National Archives)*

approached, hook down, poised to snag a wire strung across the deck – and about 29 of the options ended very, very badly.

The man in charge of managing this delicate recovery process was the landing signal officer (LSO). Stationed at the port side of the stern of the carrier, the LSO would signal the approaching pilots using a pair of aluminum paddles covered with brightly colored cloth, giving the aviators information regarding their speed and placement for an ideal landing. By following the LSO's directions, pilots could avoid some of the most dangerous predicaments. (Approaching too low and slow was often considered the most deadly corner a pilot could paint himself into.)

Two of the LSO's hand signals were mandatory for flyers. They were considered orders that had to be obeyed. The first was a "wave-off," signaled by an LSO by waving his paddles over his head. It meant something was not right with the approach or the condition of the carrier deck. Pilots were expected to add power to establish a climb, pass to the port side of the ship, and re-enter the pattern for another try.

The second was the "cut" signal, which came at the conclusion of a successful approach. To communicate this signal, the LSO lowered his left paddle and pulled the right one in front of his throat. The pilot was expected to promptly bring the throttle back to idle, point the nose downward, and then almost immediately pull back on the stick to re-establish a nose-high attitude when making contact with the deck.

The arresting hook on the aircraft would catch one of the series of wires strung across the deck, thus stopping the aircraft quickly, in the space of a few short yards. There was no "go-around" procedure; once a pilot was given the cut signal, he was coming down somewhere "in the spaghetti," as the Naval aviators were fond of saying.

Forward of the series of nine arresting wires were Davis barriers, sometimes called "crash barriers." These units held similar cables, but at heights of up to 36 inches. The barricades helped protect the men and equipment farther forward on the deck by forcibly stopping any aircraft that bounced or glided over the arresting wires.

When an aircraft "trapped" safely amid the arrestor wires, the Davis barriers were briefly dropped to allow the newly arrived plane to taxi forward. The barriers were then re-set for the next aircraft, which was already approaching.

At busy times, the LSO and deck crewmen could be recovering more than one plane every minute. The rapid pace demanded that every man involved, including the pilots, work as quickly as possible to clear the deck for the next aircraft, already poised to land. As one safety pamphlet warns, "If you are slow, the plane behind you may have to take a wave-off – and the last plane to come aboard may run out of fuel and go into the water. The last man may be you, some time."

Off the stern of Casablanca, the LSO and crewmen watch helplessly as a Hellcat fighter flops into the waves. The plane approached the carrier too slowly, the pilot lost control, and the heavy fighter "spun in." (National Archives)

THE LANDING CONTINUED

As a Hellcat wallows after a wave-off, the LSO sprints across the Cabot's deck to get out of the way of the imminent catastrophic crash. Commonly, the LSO would dive into a net situated below his platform on the port side of the deck. However, in this case the VF-29 fighter, clawing for air, appears to be headed that way, calling for an alternate escape plan. (National Museum of Naval Aviation)

Aboard Yorktown, LSO Dick Tripp gives the cut signal to an approaching aviator. Much admired, Tripp had a knack for bringing in planes, including Charles Crommelin's nearly impossibly damaged Hellcat. As one admiring SB2C flyer said, "The guy was damned near magic. Dick Tripp, for my money, was the best LSO in the whole Pacific." (National Archives)

After one Hellcat "trapped" aboard Belleau Wood, another F6F-5 came in close behind. In a second of indecision, the LSO gave the cut signal and then a wave-off. The landing pilot followed the first signal – considered an order for flyers. He touched down before the other Hellcat had completely cleared the landing area. The result of the mix-up, which happened on February 11, 1945, is seen here. H. J. Westcott, pilot of the first Hellcat, was killed. (National Museum of Naval Aviation)

When landing on the Yorktown, *this damaged F6F-3 collided with the ship's 5-inch gun turret, flying apart on impact. Lt. Bob Black's fighter was hit by gunfire over Palau on March 30, 1944. After the crash, Black walked away without a scratch. (Naval Historical Center)*

The gamble to make the vessels visible at night did have the slim potential for disaster, but it was nearly guaranteed to save the lives of many flyers milling about in the blackened skies.

Even with this concession, the process of recovering aircraft in their dire state was a disaster. A Helldiver pilot, flying on fumes, ignored a wave-off signal on the *Lexington*, bounced the barrier and plowed into another recently arrived aircraft. Despite a short-lived fire (there was hardly any gas), the *Lex* was recovering more aircraft minutes later.

The LSO on the *Enterprise* was bringing in planes so fast that a Dauntless wrenched to a stop only an inch or two from the tail of a Hellcat as it was clearing the landing area. Seconds later, another Dauntless hit the barrier and crushed itself against the carrier's island. Miraculously, the plane's pilot and gunner walked away unharmed. Later, a battle-damaged Avenger slid to a stop with crushed landing gear, closing the deck once again.

On the *Bunker Hill*, an Avenger pilot ignored a wave-off and desperate warning flares, crashing straight into an upended Helldiver, killing two of the men working to clear the original crash.

Later, sailors called the frantic night "The World's Fair," with bursting star shells, searchlight beams slicing the skies, gas-starved aircraft hitting the water, and a

Drifting too far to the right during landing, this TBM has cracked its wing on the island structure of Altamaha *in April 1944. Still dragging its crushed starboard wing, the bomber has been whirled completely around by the violence of the crash. Note the white aerial rockets strewn along the escort carrier's deck. (National Archives)*

This F6F-3 Hellcat, assigned to VF-5, overturned in the barrier of Yorktown *on April 19, 1944. An aviation mechanic would instantly start to notice what it would take to get the plane back in flying condition. At the least, repairs will have to be made to the crushed cowling, gouged leading edge, twisted pitot tube, and propeller. (National Archives)*

confused mass of desperate flyers looking for a safe place to land amid the nearly constant wrecks.

One flyer mistook a destroyer's lights for those of a carrier and made a neat landing in the water alongside the vessel. *Yorktown* sailors claim that two Helldivers, crowding each other out for the pattern, bore down on their LSO, Dick Tripp, nearly simultaneously. The unflappable signal officer coaxed one to land slightly long, and then gave the other the cut signal early, recovering both of them safely.

When morning came, the deck of the *Yorktown* was a typical scene after the night's confusion. There was an *Enterprise* SBD, four *Yorktown* Hellcats, six *Bataan* fighters,

four *Hornet* F6Fs, and one Hellcat each from *Lexington*, *Belleau Wood*, and *Bunker Hill*. An Avenger from *Hornet* and a pair of its own Helldivers rounded out the ragtag collection.

Nearly half of the 216 American aircraft participating in the evening attack during the Battle of the Philippine Sea had gone into the water. Drawing the ire of flyers already fed up with the Helldiver, it instantly became well known around the fleet that 43 of the 51 bombers didn't come back, mostly due to fuel starvation. The losses for the groups still flying the Dauntless were much lower. One of the 27 SBDs was destroyed in combat, with three more lost in crashes or ditchings.

THE BEAST

The Curtiss SB2C Helldiver entered combat on November 11, 1943. Touted as the replacement to the well-loved Douglas SBD Dauntless, the Helldiver was a step in the wrong direction according to many doubting pilots.

Airmen joked that the Helldiver's designation, SB2C, stood for "Son of a Bitch, Second Class." Others called the plane "the Big-Tailed Beast," often shortened to simply "The Beast."

The Helldiver was born with ugly traits that were a nightmare for a dive bomber – handling and stability problems, buffeting in dives, and structural weakness. The prototype Helldiver crashed repeatedly. The first accident was due to engine failure on February 8, 1941. The plane was cracked in two. Months later, when the rebuilt and improved XSB2C-1 was ready to fly again, it tore apart in mid-air when pulling out of a dive. The test pilot, Barton

Hulse, parachuted to safety as the shattered pieces of the new dive bomber fluttered to earth – a total write-off.

Later in the Pacific, the new plane's woes continued. As the first SB2Cs were flown into combat from Bunker Hill, the squadron's worried and frustrated commander reported that the SB2Cs showed little improvement from their trusty Douglas SBDs. In fact, if he had a choice, he felt much safer in the older SBD.

During the Battle of the Philippine Sea, 51 SB2Cs were launched for a long-range strike on a Japanese carrier force, along with 27 SBDs. An appalling 43 of the Curtiss dive bombers never returned. Some were lost in combat but many more were destroyed in fuel-starved ditchings. The losses for the veteran Douglas SBDs during the same mission totaled four.

The flyers found the Helldiver sluggish and heavy, often sinking below the level of the carrier deck on takeoff

On D-Day over Iwo Jima, February 19, 1945, a Curtiss SB2C cruises the skies nearby after delivering its bombs. Note the hastily painted white stripe on the right wing and tail, denoting the dive bomber is from Hancock. The geometric symbols were ordered applied to Navy planes in late January 1945. (National Archives)

when loaded with fuel and bombs. At the other end of the carrier, a landing Curtiss SB2C had noticeably less aileron control as its speed dropped below 90 knots. And the average landing speed was around 85 knots.

Gunning the engine to get out of a bad landing situation only caused new horrors – the Helldiver often pitched or stalled. Here, every square inch of the bomber's comically large rudder was put to use to keep the Helldiver's pilot and gunner out of the drink. Rumors made the rounds that the Helldiver's design had been perfect until the fuselage was shortened to make the behemoth fit on existing carrier elevators.

Despite The Beast's difficulties, it became a fundamental part of the Navy's airpower punch in the last year of the war. Helldivers were used to patrol Japanese waters and hit targets in the home islands as the hold on the Empire tightened. The planes were also instrumental in the sinking of two of the largest warships of World War II, the Japanese battleships Musashi and Yamato.

In later versions, some of The Beast's worst problems were resolved or at least nullified. There were even some aviators who loved the monstrosity. Other difficulties were harder to fix. In retrospect, Curtiss-Wright was a company in decline. On top of the design difficulties, flyers say the Helldivers suffered from poor workmanship and an erratic electrical system.

In wartime, the government needed Curtiss, even though several of the big company's military projects yielded negligible results. With Curtiss's outdated Army fighters, the company's sometimes-faulty engines, and the less-than-stellar SB2C, the airplane manufacturer didn't last long after the war ended.

In fact, some SB2Cs stuck around longer than the company, briefly flying with the post-war U.S. Navy and with French forces in Indochina into the 1950s. Other Helldivers served with Italy, Greece, Thailand, and Portugal.

The remains of a mangled SB2C are pulled from the waters somewhere stateside. The caption affixed to the photo said that the big machine was piloted by a 20-year-old "freckled kid from Wisconsin" named Larson. The caption writer also states that all the searchers were able to find of the pilot after the crash were his leg and flight-suit belt. (National Museum of Naval Aviation)

Frozen on film at flying attitude, this VB-6 Helldiver hit the crash barrier, most likely aboard the Makassar Strait in 1944. The plane has tilted up, hung for a moment, and now is crashing back down to the deck with propeller mangled and the barrier cables limp around its wheels. (National Museum of Naval Aviation)

This SB2C-3, from Hancock's VB-7, attempted a landing after dark on the deck of the Intrepid on October 29, 1944. The result of the wild night can be seen the day after – when crews begin the work of dislodging the wayward Helldiver. (National Museum of Naval Aviation)

The Helldiver, plastered against the island structure of Tarawa, contains Ens. Brown, judged by the caption writer to be "the most misunderstood ensign in the Navy…so he says." Astoundingly, the writer also says that Brown walked away from the incredibly rough landing with only a few scratches. (National Museum of Naval Aviation)

A big-tailed Helldiver came home with a large portion of its rudder missing on May 20, 1944. The SB2C-1C was photographed in the landing pattern above Essex and again when Lt. James Barnit and Airman 3rd Class Herbert Stienkmeyer had safely landed, concluding their eventful raid on Marcus Island. (National Museum of Naval Aviation and National Archives)

Photographed as it falls off the deck of an escort carrier, this FM-2 missed the wires and charged toward the bow. As deck crewmen scattered, the port wing of the passing fighter sliced through the tail and cockpit of the Wildcat parked in the foreground. Parts of the planes fill the air as the FM-2 coasts into the water. (National Museum of Naval Aviation)

Despite the horrific aircraft loss rate, portions of the American fleet picked up many of the flyers that went into the water in the days after the attack. More than 100 men came back to their carriers, soaked and cold, but ready to fly again. Another 49 weren't so lucky. They were lost during the fight, in crashes, or never found.

On October 25, 1944, flyers from a group of six escort carriers had their chance for heroics when they found themselves trapped by a powerful Japanese surface force near Samar, in the central Philippines. The aircraft aboard ship were being readied for a day of supporting the landings at Leyte when an Avenger on anti-submarine patrol frantically radioed the fleet that he'd encountered a huge armada of enemy surface ships just 20 miles away.

The American force, known as Taffy 3, consisted of six escort carriers and a handful of destroyers and destroyer escorts. The TBM pilot radioed that the Japanese vessels nearing them were four columns of bigger, faster, better-armed battleships, cruisers, and destroyers. As the Avenger pilot bravely dove toward a heavy cruiser to deliver his trio of 350-pound depth bombs, meant for a submarine,

In an explosion of splinters, the engine of an F4U-1 Corsair rips loose on the deck of Charger *in May 1944. The plane came in long, missed the wires, and hit the crash barrier while in mid-bounce, flipping completely over. The plane was assigned to VOF-1. (U.S. Navy via Peter Bowers)*

The collision with the water split open the leading edge of the wing of this SB2C-3 when it crashed off **Charger** *during training on June 21, 1944. VB-82 pilot Ens. O. R. Brown climbs from the cockpit with a good-sized bump on the head. Note the life ring, thrown from the carrier as it steams past the dying Helldiver. (National Museum of Naval Aviation)*

he knew the odds were against any of the ships in Taffy 3 surviving the next few hours.

The escort carriers began to run, but they were too slow to do anything but delay their destruction. Luckily, the ships could steam into the wind as they retreated, allowing them to launch aircraft. Planes armed for battles ashore or hunting submarines were scrambled with whatever they were carrying. Some had only their machine guns while others carried general-purpose bombs that would do little damage to an armored ship. Still more

Spun around and broken apart in a rough landing, this TBM-1C rests against the island of Hornet in June 1944. The VT-2 machine was stripped of valuable parts, and then the carcass was lifted to the side of the flight deck and dumped into the sea. (National Museum of Naval Aviation)

departed with small-depth bombs refitted with contact fuses. In the confusion, one Avenger from *Gambier Bay* was launched with only 35 gallons of gas, and another was catapulted from the deck with the engine running but no crew or pilot aboard.

American destroyers bravely turned back toward the Japanese armada, laying down smoke and fighting a losing battle with their small guns and torpedoes. The audacious charge made the Japanese commanders think they were fighting American cruisers and battleships, buying time for the baby carriers and their planes as the destroyers scattered the enemy ship formations.

Planes began arriving on the scene in fragmented groups of two to five, diving on the

During raids on the Mariana Islands, this FM-2 hit the barriers aboard the Kalinin Bay and turned over. The barriers wreck the fighter, but they stop it from careening into the rows of parked planes beyond. Now, crewmen gather to remove the stricken VC-3 aircraft. This photo was taken on June 29, 1944. (National Museum of Naval Aviation)

Pitching forward on the deck of Hornet, the engine of this Curtiss SB2C broke loose and ruptured its fuel lines. From the carrier's island, crewmen watch the action. Seconds after this photo was taken, firemen begin their work to smother the flames, and rescue men move in to retrieve the aviators. The crash took place on July 3, 1944. (National Archives)

behemoths through murderous anti-aircraft fire to deliver ineffective bombs, a handful of torpedoes, rockets, and a heavy dose of machine gun fire. When the Wildcat fighter pilots had expended every bit of their ammunition, they made mock runs on the ships. Avenger flyers did the same, making torpedo runs while their bomb bays were empty.

The Americans' bag of tricks was nearly empty and nothing could stop the Japanese warships, which began to pummel the escort carriers as they came into range.

But with the small destroyers of Taffy 3 fighting like dreadnoughts, and a constant halo of fighting aircraft ringing the Japanese cruisers and battleships like angry bees for hours, the Japanese commander became nervous,

and then panicky, and then scared. At the moment when he had all the U.S. ships at his mercy, he ordered his armada to turn away.

In a predicament in which all six of the escort carriers were as good as sunk, only the *Gambier Bay* was lost to Japanese gunfire. The vicious attacks, most notably from the U.S. destroyers, resulted in the sinking of three Japanese cruisers and heavy damage to other vessels.

Sailors aboard the escorts reveled in their good fortune. Even when outnumbered and clearly in danger, the American Navy had sent the Japanese away with a bloody nose. The noose, they said, was tightening around the Japanese Empire. The Americans' great drive across the middle of the ocean could not be stopped.

Inches above the waves, an F6F-3 from the Hancock struggles to stay airborne after losing power on takeoff. Pilots always kept their canopies open during the launch and on landing, in case they had to make a quick exit from the cockpit. This VF-7 Hellcat ran into trouble on July 6, 1944. (National Archives)

With another VF-1 Hellcat still in the wires, Ens. L. L. Cyphers gets the wave-off signal aft of the Yorktown on July 11, 1944. The pilot was killed when his fighter veered left, lost altitude, and cartwheeled into the water. It was not uncommon for a pilot to be knocked out in a crash, sinking with his aircraft before the plane guard destroyer could move up to attempt a rescue. (National Archives)

The Navy often had photographers on hand to shoot grim scenes like this one in order to humble new flyers. Young aviators, thinking they were indestructible, took risks, got into trouble, and died. Ens. Douglas Andrews was killed near Klamath Falls, Oregon, flying this FM-2 Wildcat on August 9, 1944. (U.S. Navy)

Everything pauses for a moment as a wounded pilot is extricated from his Hellcat after it hit the barrier aboard the Lexington. Ens. A. A. Bauer and his plane were shot up during the Battle of Leyte Gulf on October 25, 1944. (Naval Historical Center)

The uninformed might call him a showoff, but there is nothing this FM-2 pilot wants more right now than to safely flop back down onto his tires on the deck of Casablanca. The plane was returning from a mission near Saipan when an alert photographer shot this image of the Wildcat at the apex of its sickening attempt to "turn turtle." (National Archives)

Cutting a swath through a marsh, this F6F-3 skidded to a stop near Daytona Beach, Florida, on December 5, 1944. The plane probably suffered from an engine failure, and the pilot guided the Hellcat down to a good belly landing. Now, some poor sap must figure out a way to get the mud-covered fighter back home. (National Archives)

After catapulting from Anzio, this Avenger wallowed, finally spinning in. As the TBM-1C sunk to the bottom of the Philippine Sea, the destroyer Morris scooped this three-man crew from the water. This crash took place on December 21, 1944. (Naval Historical Center)

A load of rockets bounces loose from a Hellcat during a hard landing on Essex on December 19, 1944. In the second image, ordnancemen aboard Enterprise *discard rockets jarred free from a landing F6F-3. These 5-inch high-velocity aerial rockets went into the sea on September 15, 1944. (National Archives)*

CHAPTER FIVE

THE FINALE

After staggering losses, Japan's capacity for true offensive operations was clearly gone by the beginning of 1945. However, the war in the Pacific was far from over. Many feared that battles on the island outposts would only come to an end when the long, costly fight for the Japanese mainland began.

Some of the most hopeful estimates had American Marines and soldiers storming the beaches of Kyushu, Japan's southernmost home island, in November 1945.

Determined to be ready for the anticipated carnage on Japanese soil, American factories had minted nearly 500,000 Purple Hearts for the Kyushu invasion and for the horrors to come afterward.

Hardly anyone thought there would be a surrender. The Japanese culture bred generations of warriors. To die in battle was considered an honor. American fighting men rarely saw their enemy give in. The last three years of fighting proved that the Japanese could be beaten, but it

An FM-2, running wild after missing the wires, careens into the parked planes at the forward end of the deck of Bismarck Sea. *Note how the speeding plane has knifed right through the folded starboard wing of the Wildcat parked on the left side. Some of the sawed-off portions can be seen suspended in the air over the offending fighter's port wing.* (National Archives)

always seemed to be an incredibly costly endeavor.

A recent development in the clashes between enemy defenders and America's growing naval fleet exhibited the Japanese eagerness to fight and their willingness to die. In late 1944, enemy aircraft were seen plunging headlong into Allied vessels.

Off the Philippines on October 25, 1944, a bomb-carrying Zero smashed into the flight deck of the escort carrier *St. Lo.* (CVE-63) The collision ignited the carrier's own aircraft on the hangar deck, causing an inferno fueled by the air group's store of bombs and torpedoes. Less than 40 minutes later, the *St. Lo* was gone.

Early successful attacks, sinking a handful of ships and mauling dozens more, led the Japanese to expand their "special attack units." In the view of Japan's military leaders, the sacrifice of a small group of fervid fighting men and their aircraft was a small price to pay for putting a 7,800-ton fighting ship out of action.

A *kamikaze*, or certainly, a large group of suicide planes, was incredibly difficult to stop. The speeding aircraft was an early version of a guided missile. The fact that the man in the cockpit could continually assess the situation, dodge, turn, change targets, or tactics made the arduous task of intercepting these flying bombs even more complicated.

Always an innovator, Cdr. John Thatch developed a number of systems to deal with *kamikazes*. The first component of the system was to expand the footprint of the naval task force to allow plenty of warning. Radar-equipped destroyers and destroyer escorts ranged far out from the main forces, particularly on the sides where an attack might come. Picket ships, perhaps 50 to 60 miles out, gave enough warning to get fighters into the area to sniff out the threat.

Pickets also functioned to "delouse" incoming groups of American aircraft. A short meeting over a destroyer assured that no weary TBM flyer had an unwanted Zero or two in tail as he headed for the deck of his carrier.

The second aspect of the system to defeat *kamikazes* was simply to have more fighters on combat air patrol. Luckily, by late 1944, the Corsair was cleared for carrier duty. Along with masses of Hellcats, the F4Us helped pounce on threatening aircraft before they reached the prime targets – the carriers.

As vessels went to sea with proportionately more Corsairs and Hellcats, pilots, mechanics, and commanders learned to use the fighters for more types of jobs. When not in the role of protector, the planes were equipped with

When it slid into the parked planes on Petrof Bay *on January 29, 1945, this TBM-1C was cracked in half. The damaged VC-76 aircraft powered through the barriers, stopping only when it hit another Avenger, mashing its tail. The* Petrof Bay's *lucky shamrock insignia seems to have worked – none of the flyers were hurt in the accident. (National Museum of Naval Aviation)*

The only time there was a break in the pattern was right before sundown, and some carriers such as the *Enterprise* and *Independence* were beginning to fill that gap with night fighters.

The new systems were in place when the Navy put the small island of Iwo Jima in its sights for February 1945. Just 750 miles from Tokyo, the pre-invasion "big blue blanket" ranged up to Japan's capital. For the first time since Doolittle's attack in 1942, American planes buzzed over Tokyo.

Navy aircraft bombed and strafed targets on February 16 and part of the next day, occasionally mixing it up with Japanese fighters. As the U.S. ships steamed back towards Iwo Jima, they marveled at the success of their anti-*kamikaze* methods. Though partly protected by bad weather, in the two days, just 60 miles off Honshu, they were not threatened by any suicide aircraft.

On the evening of February 21, off Iwo Jima, things changed. The escort carrier *Bismarck Sea* was hit and sunk by *kamikazes,* and other vessels were damaged. *Saratoga* absorbed numerous vicious strikes from bombs and suicide aircraft just as the ship was launching night fighters. The battle-scarred *Sara* retreated for repairs.

bombs and rockets for attack duty alongside Avengers and Helldivers.

This helped to complete the third portion of the plan to lessen the *kamikaze* threat. While Thatch planned for defensive pickets and patrols, he encouraged more aggressive tactics as well. The "big blue blanket" concept allowed aircraft to be hammering nearby Japanese airfields nearly all day long, never allowing the enemy much time to launch aircraft.

This nearly constant coverage was a fortunate result of America's rise in carrier strength. In past actions, half the aircraft on a carrier would be used to strike, while the other half was held back as protection. Now, each of the 15 or more U.S. flattops could divide their planes into three strike groups, shuttling them to likely targets in an almost constant stream.

The final step in America's island-hopping campaign was disturbingly close to the anticipated wasp's nest of suicide planes based on Japan's home islands. Okinawa was just 350 air miles from Kyushu. Certainly, the big blue blanket would have to work overtime to cover the massive fleet of ships arrayed to deploy U.S. forces on this last bastion of enemy forces before the final, terrible conflict.

However, to nullify the *kamikaze* threat, commanders had to once again put carriers in harm's way. And this time, they were spotted early. On March 18, the hunting was bad at airfields around Kyushu – the Japanese had moved their planes away in anticipation of the attack. Counterattacks came, but the well-protected carriers escaped any serious damage.

*In a terrible crash, an SB2C-4E Helldiver assigned to VB-85 hit the barriers of **Shangri La** during a high bounce and folded up into a ball. The gunner, still strapped into his rear gun mount, was dropped onto the deck as the plane ripped apart. The accident took place on February 3, 1945. (National Museum of Naval Aviation)*

chain reaction that should have sent *Franklin* to the bottom.

Huge fires on the flight and hangar decks were fueled by the flattop's own weaponry. The blasts and horrific fires went on for hours after the attack. Tiny Tim anti-shipping rockets went skittering over the flight deck, and rivers of burning gasoline went sloshing through below-deck compartments. Explosions and fires killed hundreds of men. The flames drove many more, trapped, to jump into the sea.

With amazing tenacity, the remaining men of the *Franklin* fought back, assisted by nearby vessels. Dead in the water and burning furiously, the carrier took on a 13-degree list. The wounded vessel had no radio communications and was still dangerously close to Japan. Historians later claimed the *Franklin* was the most damaged American ship to survive afloat, and it was in much worse shape than many vessels that had previously been abandoned by their crews and sunk.

A disproportionate number of the men lost on the *Franklin* disaster were those associated with the aircraft. The initial attack wiped out most of the pilots and air crewmen waiting to take off on the deck. Many more of them were sitting in the ready rooms below the flight deck where the bombs hit. In the fire, much of the flight deck and hangar deck crews, along with the arresting gear men, ordnance handlers, and firefighters, perished at their posts.

The next morning, the Navy flyers set out to concentrate on hitting shipping, which allowed the Japanese airfields a brief respite. Suicide planes were soon in the air, their pilots searching for flattops. An attacking plane released a bomb that pierced the flight deck of *Wasp* and set off an aircraft parked below. Despite explosions and fire that led to the loss of more than 100 men and injuries to 269 more, the carrier was recovering aircraft 50 minutes later.

Damage to *Franklin*, about 50 miles off the coast of Honshu, was much worse. With fully loaded and fueled aircraft on the deck for launch, a pair of Japanese bombs came down out of an overcast sky and set off a

EARNING WINGS

In 1940, there were only some 2,500 U.S. Navy and Marine Corps pilots on active duty. In the next five years, an astonishing 59,000 additional airmen would be taught to fly "the Navy way" at airfields throughout the country.

The training programs were a strange combination of urgency and cautious prudence. While scores of Navy airmen were needed immediately in the Pacific, they had to be skilled flyers, expected to perform in combat right away. There was no sense in sending unprepared recruits to simply perish. The Navy needed experts in navigation, airmanship, and combat. Anything less was a wasteful depletion of lives and machines.

As a result, the training regimen stayed strict, difficult, and time-consuming. The first stop on a student's journey to the role of pilot was the "E base," or Flight Elimination Base. Here, instructors taught the basics of aviation. After around 10 hours of schooling, a student soloed. Or he was sent packing.

If the Navy found that a cadet was worth keeping, the next step was primary flight training. At primary schools, the skies were always buzzing with prospective pilots, commonly at the controls of Stearman N2S biplane trainers, nicknamed "Yellow Perils." The brilliant yellow airplanes helped cadets see one another in the crowed skies and were easy to spot when they came down in a farmer's pasture. To experienced airmen, the sight of a Yellow Peril was a visual warning, as if to say, "Look out, I'm a beginner and there's no telling what I might do up here."

The Stearmans had to be rugged. Students bounced, stressed, and spun them in every conceivable way. They were often able to stand a beating and keep flying – or, at least, be repaired a few hours after flipping over, dragging a wing, or stalling out a few feet too high over the runway.

Most who "washed out" of primary did so by failing to show quick progress or the skills necessary to continue training. But a few went by the wayside in accidents. Instructors commented that very new flyers hardly ever got into serious trouble. But those who were deemed notoriously hopeless were watched very carefully.

Amid legions of beautiful Stearman N2S-3 Kaydets, a student flyer ambles in from a solo flight. The basic trainers were built simple and sturdy in order to take (most of) whatever a fledgling flyer could throw their way and keep on flying. (U.S. Navy via Peter Bowers)

In early 1942, this N2S-1 dropped out of the skies over Pensacola and smashed into a landing field at a steep angle. The wreck killed the instructor in the rear seat and the young student up front. It is unknown who was flying at the time. (National Archives)

Conversely, overconfidence caused some of the worst crashes, they said. It was the student who showed promise and "lulled an instructor to sleep" who was the dangerous one. Or later, flying solo, it was the cadet who liked to squeeze under bridges or harass cars on the highway who often ended his flying career in a smoldering mess of splintered wood and twisted metal. Safety brochures constantly reminded flyers: "Naval aviation is **not** a sport – it is a scientific profession."

As an airman moved on to basic and then advanced training, he flew increasingly bigger, heavier, and more complex craft, like the Vultee SNVs and North American SNJs. One cadet recalls an admiral telling his class, "I'm going to give you three rules for

Near Ottumwa, Iowa, a pair of N2S primary trainers met, nose to nose. Perhaps it is a testament to the uniformity of Navy flying to see how each pilot reacted. Both planes' left wings took the brunt of the blow as the flyer swerved, and the machines ended up as mirror images of one another on the tarmac after the collision. (National Museum of Naval Aviation)

EARNING WINGS CONTINUED

a long life as a pilot. The first rule is airspeed. And the second rule? Well, the second rule is airspeed." The third rule, of course, was the same. Airspeed. Keep moving and it's possible to fly out of all sorts of sticky situations.

It was one of the two major requirements for flying "the Navy way." Precise control of speed, along with crisp and well-executed maneuvers, was what it took to land a 12-ton flying boat at sea or return to the storm-swept deck of a tiny carrier. If a pilot forgot his training, he was likely to get wet – or much, much worse.

RBME-805-1   22 FEB 1945
CRASH N2S-5   FIELD 21
Bu #43531   STA # 211

Overturned near a training base close to Memphis, Tennessee, this Stearman N2S-5 Kaydet awaits recovery. The plane flipped over when the student pilot "stood on the brakes." Note how the plane's Lycoming engine was bent downward and how the plane's right upper wing was smashed against the concrete in the middle of the flip. (U.S. Navy via Peter Bowers)

A photographer captures a shot of an SNJ-6 from Corry Field, Florida, as it was put back on its gear. The plane went over in a very rough landing on December 13, 1943. Working into the night, crewmen have just gotten the training aircraft righted, and will soon bring in a flatbed truck to take the plane back to base. The flyer at the controls was not seriously hurt in the accident. (National Museum of Naval Aviation)

CLEAR THE DECK!

In the last stages of training, student flyers handled larger, more powerful aircraft. The North American SNJ-3 trainer usually helped soon-to-be aviators learn to fly fighters. This one was drilled into the ground in an accident too terrible to walk away from. This mangled aircraft lies in the woods near Jacksonville, Florida, in late 1942. (National Archives)

Here, a flyer cuts his carrier aviation career short before it really got started. During a practice landing on Monterey in 1953, a student lets an SNJ-5C get away from him on final approach and pays dearly. The flyer was killed in the accident. The aircraft was from the basic carrier qualification class based at Barin Field, Alabama. (National Museum of Naval Aviation)

Looking down from the island of the Bennington, a brave photographer captured this stark image of a Corsair burning on the flight deck below. This accident took place on February 14, 1945. (National Museum of Naval Aviation)

With its tail hook clawing for a wire, an F6F-5N night fighter hits the barrier while landing on Sangamon on February 26, 1945. The VF-33 Hellcat, flown by Lt. William Bailey, burst into flames moments after impact. The caption with the image reports that the pilot escaped unhurt and also states that the fighter was repaired and flew again. (Naval Historical Center)

The final toll was 724 dead. The last body was uncovered amid the twisted wreckage as the battered and scorched carrier pulled into New York Harbor on April 28, 1945.

After the attacks on the home island airfields, the invasion of Okinawa began on April 1, 1945. As the fight ashore progressed, the Japanese funneled hundreds of planes into the area, conducting both conventional and suicide attacks on the American ships supporting the invasion.

Nearly 700 enemy planes converged on Okinawa on April 6. Despite frantic efforts to keep the Japanese attackers at bay, the suicide planes succeeded in crashing into 19 vessels, sinking a handful of destroyers and merchant ships and damaging scores of others.

To the north, another suicide mission began that same day. On April 6, submarines lurking off the coast of Japan spotted a fleet of Japanese ships steaming toward Okinawa. Along with the eight destroyers and a cruiser

sailed *Yamato* – the largest battleship in the world. The 72,800-ton vessel had nine 18.1-inch main guns that could fire 3,200-pound shells.

In a desperate attempt to disrupt the landings at Okinawa, Japan's military leaders sent the massive

Commonly, there are large groups of men out on the island of a carrier, watching the planes land. Aboard Prince William, *if anyone was watching, they are now cowering under the railing. An F4U-1D assigned to VBF-84 bashed into the island after a missed approach and the nose section stuck, nearly vertically, against the structure. The burning Corsair snapped almost in half at the cockpit, trapping the injured flyer. Fire crews were on the scene within moments to smother the flames. The crash took place on February 24, 1945. (National Museum of Naval Aviation)*

warship and its crew of 2,767 on a one-way trip. After ripping into the American fleet nearby, the captain had orders to beach the great battleship offshore, creating an unsinkable gun emplacement.

It was a flawed plan from the start. *Yamato's* strike force was comparatively small, and the vessels had no air cover. America's skilled and eager carrier aviators, many of whom were training during the days when

Japan ruled the seas, practically jumped at the chance to hammer the remnants of the Imperial Japanese Navy.

The next day, a plane from the *Essex* spotted the great ship and escorts. Avenger crews on the *Yorktown* cheered when ordered to load torpedoes into the bellies of their planes – it had been months since any of them had carried anything but bombs.

OVER THE SIDE

It was shocking to veteran sailors, who remembered how, in peacetime, the miserly Navy had treated every plane, even a wrecked one, like it was gold. Now, deck crews often quickly pushed damaged planes over the side. A carrier deck was no junkyard. If the offending aircraft couldn't be repaired quickly and easily, it was simply taking up valuable space. It was a hazard. The industrial might of the United States could build another. An aircraft too damaged to repair was simply in the way.

If time allowed, mechanics attacked the doomed machine with their tools, piling up a mass of useful, undamaged parts: wheels and tires, radio, instruments, hinges, doors, Plexiglas, guns – whatever was needed and whatever could be torn free quickly.

Sooner than they wanted, the deck crane was in position and sailors affixed cables. Other crewmen chopped holes in the plane's skin to make it sink faster.

When fuel-starved aircraft returned to the fleet in treacherous weather or at night, they sometimes landed on the first carrier available. One frantic evening, Yorktown recovered its own planes and many more.

With fighters and bombers parked everywhere, and more arriving by the minute, the captain quickly gave the order to "deep six" perfectly good aircraft to make more room. Saving the life of a Navy pilot was valued much more than retaining a plane. One carrier crewman mused that one trained pilot was worth at least 20 planes.

Sailors on carriers like Belleau Wood were happy to know that their missing pilots were safe on another vessel, but more than a little miffed that their perfectly good Hellcats had been chosen to be wrestled over to the deck-edge elevator and tumbled into the sea. The only thing saved from the relatively new 5-ton fighters before they went into the drink was their eight-day clocks – valuable souvenirs that went to the quick-thinking and even quicker-working Yorktown crewmen.

The condemned aircraft hit the water with a thud. The lifeguard rescue destroyer trailing the carrier made a brief course correction to bypass the sinking carcass. Alone at sea, the flying machine eventually slipped beneath the waves, diving through five miles of sunless sea to one final landing on the ocean floor.

A General Motors TBM is committed to the deep after a short funeral service for the gunner, killed in action in combat near the Philippines on January 4, 1945. The flyer's body was left inside the turret of the flak-damaged Avenger, and the entire irreparable bomber was shoved off the stern. (Northrop Grumman)

A "dud" TBM-1C gets a final chance to briefly speed through the sky after being raided for useful parts. The plane, from VC-79 on Sargent Bay, was shot up in a mission over Iwo Jima on February 25, 1945. Crewmen have punched hundreds of holes in the bomber's skin to assure that it sinks quickly after it is launched from the catapult. (National Archives)

An F4U-4 from Hancock is lifted by a deck crane, which will move it close to the edge for its final drop into the sea. The VBF-6 fighter-bomber was judged too time-consuming to repair after it was damaged in an accident in mid-1945. Crewmen have taken the time to strip many useful parts, including the wheels, canopy, and gear doors. (National Museum of Naval Aviation)

An Essex Hellcat, mangled in a barrier accident, is craned over to the side for disposal. With both wings battered, nose caved in, and tail fractured, the plane is nearly useless – a dangerous liability. Soon enough, the carrier will be resupplied with a new F6F. (U.S. Navy via Paul Madden)

After bringing its pilot home to Block Island, this shot-up Hellcat was judged too damaged to fix and was dumped into "Davy Jones' Locker." This Grumman F6F's flying career ended with an unceremonious shove sometime in May 1945 near Okinawa. (The Museum of Flight/Taylor Collection)

This F6F-3 Hellcat assigned to VF-6 was heavily damaged in a landing accident and resulting fire aboard Belleau Wood on October 6, 1943. (National Museum of Naval Aviation)

The burned shell of the fighter is being coaxed overboard. Note that the tail, cracked in the crash, has been totally torn from the aircraft. A few ingenious sailors are employing a pole to help lever the plane into the drink. (National Museum of Naval Aviation)

An F6F-5 Hellcat jerks to a stop after a rough landing on Lexington. The VF-9 aircraft was still carrying its belly tank, which slid forward and was sliced by the propeller. This series of photos shows the resulting inferno and the pilot's quick escape down the right wing. The accident happened on February 25, 1945. (National Museum of Naval Aviation)

The third F6F-3 to land on **Solomons** on May 3, 1945, missed the wires, jumped the barriers, and hurtled into the planes parked on the forward edge of the deck. In a shower of twisted aircraft pieces, at least two of the three aircraft pitched over the bow. Note the crewman, putting the chalks around the right tire of number 56, seemingly unaware of the danger until it was right on top of him. (National Archives)

While attacking targets on Chi Chi Jima on March 3, 1945, this TBM-3 collided with another flak-blasted Avenger. Using all of his strength, the pilot was able to keep the grievously damaged VT-82 bomber under control and fly home. Unwilling to even consider landing on the deck of Bennington, the flyer ditched nearby. All three crewmen were rescued. (Naval Historical Center)

A few of the deck crewmen on Suwannee watch, almost impassively, as an F6F-5 falls into the sea after the pilot lost his struggle to gain flying speed on takeoff. There is really nothing they can do to help. The man on the left drags a bridle, used to attach the plane to the catapult mechanism in the carrier's deck. (National Archives)

Other planes arrived on the scene before the *Yorktown's* aircraft. At 12:32 PM, the first of a long stream of hundreds of blue combat planes spotted their targets and dove in. *Yamato's* 18.1-inch cannons boomed, followed by hundreds of smaller caliber guns. The first bombs, from *Bennington's* Helldivers, exploded near the battleship's main mast at 12:41 PM

More torpedoes and bombs followed as the additional Navy planes swooped in on the battleship and its escorts. Fires burned on *Yamato's* deck and the ship took on a list, but the armored monster kept going. There were even a few pilots who began to doubt that the weaponry carried by the planes could actually sink the great dreadnought.

While the Japanese vessels had no air cover, they continued to put up terrific barrages of anti-aircraft fire. Many aircraft collected bullet holes and shrapnel scars, yet few went down. The fight was decidedly one-sided as the great ship tilted more and more to port, lifting its armor-belted waterline and exposing its venerable underbelly.

Six Avenger torpedo planes from the *Yorktown* lumbered out of the overcast just as the nearby cruiser in the Japanese force was consumed by smoke and flames, overturned, and went under.

Lt. Thomas Stetson led his flyers toward *Yamato's* exposed right side, down on the deck at 300 miles per hour. The Avengers dropped their "fish" in the water as the battleship veered to the left, but they released their weapons at can't-miss range. Blasts rocked the massive ship as the torpedoes fractured hull plating and hurled pieces of the ship into the sea.

Minutes later, *Yamato* rolled over on its side and exploded, throwing fire and debris thousands of feet into the sky. A huge black column of smoke rose into the air for miles, the tiny carrier planes still swarming around it.

In one way, the end of *Yamato* signaled the end of all battleships. Even those who ignored Pearl Harbor had to admit that the aircraft carrier and its complement of aviators and planes could take on anything afloat. The defeat of the leviathan and her escorts had cost the Navy 10 planes and 12 flyers.

The great ship was also the symbol of an entire nation. When *Yamato* died, along with the majority of its crew, it signified the end of Japan as a naval power – the end of Japan as the dominant force in the Pacific.

Into May and June, the carriers worked to cover the activities at Okinawa from Japanese air attack. Over time, Army and Navy units ashore were able to take over the job of blanketing nearby airfields to keep the Empire's aviators at bay.

The fleet found itself preparing for one final, grim campaign. Come November, every carrier and every flyer would be needed to overcome resistance as thousands of young Marines and soldiers went ashore.

The aviators occupied their time pouncing on shipping, scouting military activities, and raiding airfields and ports. August 15, 1945, started like any other day for the carrier flyers. They were up early hauling bombs, droning toward Atsugi, Kure, or downtown Tokyo.

When word came over the radio at around 6:45 AM, each aircraft dumped its bombs into the water. The war was over. Then the great formations of carrier aircraft turned back into the rising morning sun and headed for home.

An Avenger, trailing a thick band of smoke, heads toward Essex after catching a dose of anti-aircraft fire over Okinawa. The crew of Essex had a reputation for taking damaged aircraft aboard when no one else would take the chance. This plane was hit on March 28, 1945. (Naval Historical Center)

Near Iwo Jima, an FM-2 Wildcat runs into trouble while approaching Sargent Bay in March 1945. The VC-83 Wildcat came in too low, and when the pilot "poured on the coals," the little fighter fell off on its left wing. There is nothing the men in the escort carrier's catwalk can do but hope the pilot gets out unharmed. (National Museum of Naval Aviation)

After returning to Langley, Ens. George Bailey was asked to pose next to the shot-up tail of his F6F-5. Near Kikai Shima, the flyer tangled with Japanese Ki-61 Tony fighters. The action took place on April 11, 1945. Though it nearly turned out to be a bad day for the young Hellcat flyer, he still managed a smile. (National Museum of Naval Aviation)

An FM-2 is captured in mid-flip after hitting the barriers on the Petrof Bay *on April 16, 1945. The alert photographer snapped this image as the tail buries itself in the deck. The nose is still suspended in the air. Most amazing of all, the plane's belly fuel tank is seen in the air, gushing gas, at the upper left-hand portion of the frame. (National Archives)*

Hopelessly burned when its belly tank caught fire on landing, an F6F Hellcat was promptly hooked up for a catapult shot. The flash-cooked fighter was flung off the deck of Nehenta Bay *on May 7, 1945, its engine silent and its cockpit empty – a quick way to dispose of the unwanted machine. (National Archives)*

This Avenger was attempting a landing on the evening of April 16, 1945, aboard Solomons. During a wave-off, the TBM-1C clipped the carrier's mast with its right wing, causing the big bomber to spin out of control and scrape its tail on the edge of the flight deck as it hurdled into the water. The plane was nearly out of fuel, so it floated well. Here, the pilot can be seen on the wing, moving back to assist his crew. (National Archives)

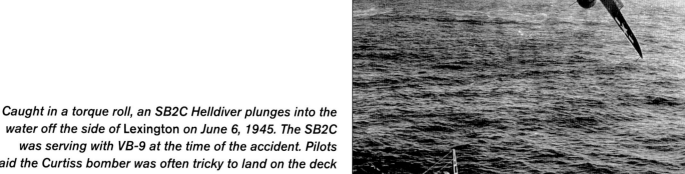

Caught in a torque roll, an SB2C Helldiver plunges into the water off the side of Lexington on June 6, 1945. The SB2C was serving with VB-9 at the time of the accident. Pilots said the Curtiss bomber was often tricky to land on the deck of a carrier. (National Museum of Naval Aviation)

After its hook snapped, this VF-12 Hellcat veered off the port side of Randolph on April 18, 1945. When the fighter's right wing hit the barrier post, the plane turned over and dove into the water. Ens. W. L. Mason, the pilot, was killed in the accident. (National Museum of Naval Aviation)

In the intense heat, the skin of this Hellcat from Randolph buckles on April 22, 1945. When the propeller struck the plane's fuel tank, a massive conflagration flared up immediately. At first, Ens. Lowell Rund couldn't escape, and deck crewmen were unable to get to him as he huddled in the cockpit. Luckily, the fire died down quickly, and Rund was able to clamber to safety. The pilot suffered from third-degree burns on his neck and lesser burns on his face and shoulders. (National Archives)

WEATHERING THE STORM

Sailors and aviators complained that the weather on the open sea was hardly ever good. It was an exaggeration. Navy men have always been prone to overstatement.

However, in wartime there was often no avoiding a squall, a gale, or sometimes even a typhoon. Everyone on board the ships learned to live with the weather; from the baker who found that his cakes wouldn't rise in tossing seas, to the pilot who joked he was often sent out to fly patrols when the ceiling was below the water line.

Weather could sometimes be a savior. Carrier captains wanted clear skies for aircraft operations, but sailing near a downburst could be an easy escape if kamikazes suddenly appeared.

But more often than not, bad weather was, of course, nothing but a hardship. It meant food served cold, sleeping in a rolling bunk, and a tossing, rain-swept flight deck. One flyer spotted his escort carrier struggling through stormy seas far below, and ominously wrote, "The ship looks like a tiny nameplate on the lid of my coffin."

No matter how well they were secured, aircraft sometimes broke loose on the deck, smashing into other planes or pitching over the side. Deck crews did what they could, risking life and limb to corral a Hellcat-turned-battering ram or a wayward Dauntless with one wheel already in the catwalk.

On Hornet, one sailor recalled a big radial engine housed in a crate on the hangar deck that broke loose in high seas. Shedding its wooden container on a nearby Avenger, the one-ton wrecking ball tumbled from one bulkhead to the other, tearing into aircraft.

Even worse, as the engine rolled and slid along the steel deck, it created bright sparks. There were napalm tanks and high-explosive bombs stored everywhere on the hangar deck. Eventually, unless arrested, the situation would turn from a localized accident into a ship-wide disaster. "But finally," the sailor later wrote, "some honest-to-God hero somehow got a line on that engine, tied the rope to the bulkhead, and gradually pinned it down."

Topside, landing was tricky enough without the added dimension of a violently pitching flight deck. Sometimes the landing wires would distressingly fall away from an approaching aircraft. Other times, the deck leapt up to meet the oncoming machine, the two colliding with a bone-jarring crunch.

During high seas, a Corsair twists sideways and slides off the deck of Essex. Re-securing aircraft that had broken free during a storm was a difficult and dangerous task. Weighty and on wheels, the planes tended to shift easily, even when aggressively tied down. (U.S. Navy via Paul Madden)

After the December 18, 1944, typhoon in the Philippine Sea, deck crews on Altamaha salvage what they can from a ravaged Hellcat. Nearly half of the replacement aircraft the ship was carrying got swept overboard in the storm. This fighter, though still on the deck, didn't fare much better. The ship lost 12 Avengers, 15 Helldivers, and 16 Hellcats. (National Archives)

WEATHERING THE STORM

One day on Yorktown, a Hellcat was coming down as the deck was quickly rising up. So concerned with his tricky, rough weather landing, the pilot had forgotten to put his guns on safe. In a split second, the rapidly rising deck and descending F6F collided, the plane's external fuel tank rocketing into the whirling propeller and the fighter's six .50-caliber machine guns spitting a burst of lead. Seconds before, the carrier had been up and running. Now, the plane heaped at its stern was engulfed in flames, 11 men were wounded, and five parked aircraft ahead were damaged by flying bullets.

In the last months of war, the U.S. fleet was exposed to two typhoons in the Pacific. The first, in the Philippine Sea on December 18, 1944, overwhelmed three destroyers and heavily damaged five carriers. A report on the disaster relates, "Fires occurred in three carriers when planes broke loose in their hangars and some 146 planes on various ships were lost or damaged beyond economical repair by fires, impact damage, or by being swept overboard."

The second storm hit on June 3, 1945, east of Okinawa. Four fleet carriers and a number of escort carriers were damaged, including Yorktown and Bennington, which suffered the catastrophic collapse of their forward flight decks. In total, storm damage wrecked 43 planes, and another 33 were washed overboard.

Seen on the hangar deck of Monterey, this TBM-1C assigned to VT-28 bashed itself apart during the December 18, 1944, typhoon. Several aircraft on the hangar deck caught fire during the ordeal. In total, 18 planes were completely demolished or burned. (National Museum of Naval Aviation)

An Avenger, wings still folded, gets a final launch off the catapult of Bougainville. The torpedo bomber was irreparably damaged in the June 3, 1945, typhoon east of Okinawa. Launching the derelict aircraft was a clean, quick, and safe way to remove the unwanted plane from the deck. (National Archives)

During a typhoon, a Piper NE-1 observation plane got airborne in the 75-mile-per-hour winds and bounced along an Okinawa airfield until it hit a Marine TBM. Unable to separate the two planes in the middle of the storm, crewmen chose to lash them together. The result is seen here, after the typhoon has passed. (U.S. Navy)

CHAPTER SIX

POST-WAR

The years after World War II were difficult for the U.S. Navy. The end of hostilities brought great joy, but also new troubles. Demobilization of America's massive wartime force was the first thing on many politicians' minds. And the components of the Navy that survived the drastic cuts would be reorganized to take on new tasks.

As wartime fleets of ships and aircraft were pushing their way toward the Japanese home islands in 1945, there was a force of 3.4 million men in the Navy. A scant two years later, there were slightly more than 500,000.

The greatest seaborne force the world has ever known had more than 100 aircraft carriers in that last year of fighting. One year later, there were 25 flattops in service.

The pilot of this TBM-3E was climbing out of Boeing Field near Seattle on February 9, 1946, when the big plane's Cyclone engine quit cold. He guided the plane over a nearby neighborhood, hoping to find a clear spot to set the bomber down. His wing hit a pole, and the plane ended up on an unsuspecting family's doorstep. (National Museum of Naval Aviation)

On March 14, 1946, this Curtiss SB2C sunk sickeningly low on approach to Shangri La. A "ramp strike" followed, tearing apart the aircraft. Most of the crushed plane settled on the deck. Miraculously, the pilot is reported to have walked away from the crash unhurt. (National Archives)

Operation Crossroads allowed the military to study the effects of atomic blasts on ships and equipment, including aircraft. This Wildcat, deemed expendable, endured the blast of the 21-kiloton nuclear weapon ABLE from the deck of the attack transport Crittenden. *Two days later, on July 3, 1946, men examine the twisted fighter. (National Archives)*

For a brief moment in time, before the North Koreans came south in June 1950, the U.S. Navy possessed only nine operational fleet carriers.

Battle-scarred vessels of World War II had been mothballed, scrapped, or sold. The *Saratoga* and *Independence* were used in the atom bomb tests at Bikini Atoll in 1946.

The veteran "Stripe-Stacked *Sara*" had been commissioned in 1927, and during the war the ship had been wounded several times by Japanese torpedoes, bombs, and *kamikazes*. More than 89,000 aircraft had landed on that well-worn flight deck over the span of 19 years.

The *Sara* withstood the first atomic blast at Bikini with little damage – the carrier was stationed about four miles away. The second bomb was detonated only 500 feet from the *Sara*, sweeping all the surplus aircraft tied down on her flight deck into the lagoon in an instant. Mortally damaged and poisoned with radiation, the oldest U.S.

carrier in the Navy finally slipped beneath the waves more than seven hours later.

Not only were old carriers getting the "deep six," those being built were also fair game for destruction. The half-completed Essex class *Reprisal* was used for experiments with explosives. The unfinished *Iwo Jima* was chopped apart for scrap in its slip at Newport News.

The drastic drop in strength was alarming. Some cautioned that a butcher-block strategy had gotten the Navy into trouble in the years after World War I. Navy officials warned politicians that the budget and size of America's Naval forces could be cut, but there would soon come a day when they would regret it – a day when the Navy might be desperately needed.

In this time of budget slashing, the Navy was also struggling to incorporate a wide array of new technologies into regular service – jet aircraft, guided missiles, nuclear weapons, and helicopters.

Sometimes, a flyer takes any landing spot he can get. This Marine pilot chose the broad North Carolina beach near Cherry Point when the engine of his Corsair began to die in January 1947. Coming down upright and relatively undamaged in the soft sand was no easy trick. Now, the only question is: will the mechanics retrieve the plane before the tides do? (U.S. Marine Corps via Dick Rainforth)

This Navy chop yard in Norfolk, Virginia, is a sad sight for those who love airplanes. Machines involved in accidents or those simply worn out come to die here. Careful study of the 1948 snapshot reveals the remains of many Corsairs, Hellcats, Skyraiders, and Avengers, among others. (National Archives)

In Norfolk, Virginia, an electric guillotine hacks a Curtiss SB2C Helldiver into pieces in 1948. The aircraft-grade aluminum from thousands of old World War II-era fighting machines was being melted into ingots. (National Archives)

The rise of the jet engine, more than anything, changed aircraft-carrier design to its modern form. On July 21, 1946, the Navy's first jet aircraft, a McDonnell XFD-1 Phantom, took off and landed for the first time on a carrier deck. The carrier, *Franklin D. Roosevelt,* would be one of many flattops from the era to undergo an extensive retrofit, including new steam catapults and an angled deck to accommodate the new type of propeller-less aircraft.

The idea of carrier-borne aircraft able to deliver atomic bombs was of particular concern to those who were fighting to keep the aircraft carrier a viable and valuable weapon in the developing Cold War with the Soviet Union. The problem was, the early versions of these bombs were large and heavy. Obviously, there was no room for a big, four-engine Army-type bomber on a carrier deck.

The temporary solution was the Lockheed P2V Neptune patrol bomber that could be loaded, by crane, onto the deck of a Midway class carrier. Using its pair of piston engines and JATO rockets, the loaded Neptune could struggle into the air, fly more than 2,000 miles, deliver its deadly cargo, and, in theory, return. The return was tricky – the patrol plane was not equipped to land on the carrier deck. It would either have to ditch at sea or find a friendly airfield within the 2,000-plus mile range.

The cumbersome process was superceded by the arrival of the truly carrier-capable North American AJ-1 Savage attack bomber in the last months of 1949. The aircraft was able to operate from a carrier and deliver "the bomb" using a strange combination of two piston-powered engines, complemented by a turbojet that could be employed for extra boost on takeoff or over a hostile target.

The large sizes and heavy weights of early jets made the steam-boosted catapults a valuable addition. Upon landing, the long spool-up times of the first jet engines made alighting on a straight-decked carrier even more of an adventure than it was during the war. The angled deck, a British innovation, gave more room for error, greatly simplified flight operations for jets, and allowed aircraft to "bolter" (miss the carrier's arresting gear), and climb back into the landing pattern instead of crashing headlong into the barriers.

There were still many nonbelievers. Some military strategists argued that the carrier was too expensive and too vulnerable in an all-out war with the Soviets. A "super carrier" in the first stages of construction was cancelled, causing great anger in Navy circles. The Navy types snidely remarked that if Congress wanted to see "expensive and vulnerable," they should take a very hard look at the strategic bomber they had just agreed to fund.

Sure enough, when fighting broke out in Korea in 1950, the Convair B-36 intercontinental bomber was not a useful tool for fighting North Korean aggression. Old, rust-streaked aircraft carriers, from what many predicted

was a bygone era, proved nearly perfect for the task.

In Korea, U.S. Navy and Marine Corps aircraft flew 276,000 combat sorties from carriers, dropped 177,000 tons of bombs, and fired 272,000 rockets. It was 70,000 sorties fewer than what was flown during World War II, but the planes delivered 74,000 more tons of bombs and 60,000 more rockets in Korea.

In the first year of fighting, carrier aircraft shot down 83 enemy planes, felled 313 bridges, and obliterated 262 boats, 220 locomotives, 163 tanks, and almost 3,000 other vehicles.

By the outbreak of fighting in Korea, nearly every Navy aircraft used during World War II was gone – chopped apart to create aluminum ingots. The exceptions to the rule were squadrons of Vought Corsairs, relative latecomers to carriers flying in the Pacific. The Corsairs soldiered on, mostly with the unglamorous task of catapulting off their ships loaded with bombs, depositing them on some grubby, flak-infested North Korean target, and then returning to the carriers for more.

However, one F4U flyer from the carrier *Princeton* earned special distinction. When Guy Bordelon, flying a Corsair equipped for night fighting, shot down his fifth and final enemy aircraft on June 29, 1953, he became an ace.

Moreover, he became the only Navy's ace in Korea, the only flyer in Korea to attain the status of ace in a propeller-driven aircraft, and the only night-fighter ace during the conflict. And, in an era when the days of piston-engine combat planes were numbered, Guy Bordelon became most likely the world's last pilot to achieve the title of ace in a propeller-driven aircraft.

A wave-off went awry when a burst of power brought the left wing of this TBM-3E down hard on the deck of Tarawa. The big bomber turned completely upside down before hitting the water. This Avenger's last flight took place in December 1948. (National Archives)

Lt. Michael Stachow wrestles with his F4U-4 Corsair as it clips the deck and turns over next to Philippine Sea on January 10, 1949. Hitting nose first, the plane floated briefly with its tail high in the air. The pilot was able to climb from the cockpit. (Naval Historical Center)

Uh oh. This Hellcat caught a wire, but when the tail separates, all bets are off. Note how the crewmen at the far end of the deck begin to scatter as the wounded fighter speeds toward them and the crash barrier. This strange mishap took place on the Princeton in September 1951. (National Archives)

It was a sure bet that nothing good was going to come out of this meeting between a TBM-3C and the island structure of Siboney. The VC-31 bomber bounced high on landing, its propeller hitting a cameraman filming the action from the rear of the island. The plane's tail settled to the deck, while the nose leaned against the superstructure, pointed upwards. The pilot escaped the April 19, 1949, accident unharmed. (National Museum of Naval Aviation)

Just a fraction of a second before its plunge into the water, a TBM-3 departs the right side of the deck of Block Island. When this image was taken in late 1951 or early 1952, the Avenger was assigned to an attack squadron. (National Archives)

FORGOTTEN FIGHTERS

The designers at Grumman could not hope to "stand around and watch" as their new F6F fighter went to the Pacific in service with the U.S. Navy. Well before the first Hellcat began to tangle with a Japanese Zero, the engineers at Grumman were already working feverishly on their next designs – the planes that might potentially replace the F6F if the fighting continued into 1946 and beyond.

The dependable and powerful Pratt & Whitney R-2800 Double Wasp used in the Hellcat (and the Vought F4U Corsair and Republic P-47 Thunderbolt Army fighter) was retained for new designs. The F7F Tigercat employed a pair of the engines in a streamlined, complex airframe that was almost too large to be called a fighter. The machine could carry 2,000 pounds of bombs or a full-size torpedo.

The next creation, the F8F Bearcat, was the opposite in stature. It was Grumman's attempt to build the lightest, smallest aircraft it could around a single Double Wasp engine. The result was a fighter that, compared to the gold-standard Hellcat, was lighter, faster, could climb better, and was able to fly from the smallest carrier in the fleet.

While both the F7F and F8F were on the fast track to get into combat before the end of fighting in the Pacific, neither made it. Because of difficulties with the size of the Tigercat, the younger Bearcat was closest to the fight. Squadrons of shiny new Bearcats would have been deployed to chase down kamikaze aircraft had the war continued to Japan's doorstep. When the atomic bombs were dropped, the pint-sized machines were only weeks from joining the action.

In peacetime, the contracts signed during World War II were slashed. Bearcat production, however, continued in moderate numbers. Tigercat production halted at 364, while a total of 1,265 Bearcats emerged from Grumman's factory.

The Navy viewed the more-sprightly F8F as a useful stop-gap between the Hellcats and the jet fighters that would surely arrive soon. The Bearcats even displaced the Hellcat as the chosen fighter for the Navy's Blue Angels starting in 1946. The aircraft served with the flight demonstration team, as well as Navy front-line service, until 1950.

Bearcats were sweethearts, said pilots, fast and nimble. They were loved by nearly all who flew them, including former Navy pilot Neil Armstrong. The boys at Grumman grumbled that the little fighters were great, but

An F7F-3N Tigercat and F8F-1 Bearcat cruise the skies over New York for press photographers on April 4, 1947. Note the similarities between the two Grumman-designed fighters' tails. (The Museum of Flight/Taylor Collection)

CLEAR THE DECK!

they had arrived days too late. They never served in combat with the U.S. Navy.

France acquired some Bearcats in 1954, for use in French Indochina. Flown by French Expeditionary Force pilots, the F8Fs were used as close air-support aircraft, attacking Vietminh forces on the ground. When France withdrew, the planes were taken over by the South Vietnamese Air Force. Bearcats also flew with the Royal Thai Air Force.

The U.S. Navy and Marine Corps converted many of the less-cherished Tigercats into night fighters, attack aircraft, or photo recon planes in the years after World War II. The Tigercat's first and only time in battle came with Marine flyers during the early stages of the Korean War.

Today, both forgotten fighter types are as rare as the Navy combat planes of World War II – with only a handful of examples surviving in museums or in the hands of private owners.

Everyone, it seems, is out on the island of Randolph to see an F8F rumble into the skies in late 1951. Grumman promoted the Bearcat as having the smallest possible airframe mated to the dependable and powerful R-2800 engine. (National Archives)

Caught in a torque roll, a Bearcat assigned to VF-62 does a back flip off the deck of Coral Sea. The fighter bounced once, dragged its left wing, and dove into the drink. The crash took place while the carrier was stationed off the coast of Korea. (The Museum of Flight/Taylor Collection)

FORGOTTEN FIGHTERS CONTINUED

Fancy flying…though this Bearcat pilot is desperately struggling to achieve "straight and level." The trouble started when the VF-1A fighter bounced high on landing and the pilot jerked the stick left and back to dodge the Tarawa's rapidly approaching island structure. Without enough speed to sustain sideways flight, the F8F-1 quickly lost altitude and ended up in the water in September 1947. As the plane sank, nose first, the shaken flyer bobbed to the surface. (National Archives)

A barrier crash aboard Kearsarge tore the engine off the mounts of this Bearcat and ruptured the fighter's fuel lines. As the fire flares up, the pilot decides it is time to make his exit. Steaming briskly into the wind during aircraft-recovery operations, the carrier fans the flames as they engulf the fuselage. (National Museum of Naval Aviation)

Near Carlsbad, California, a Tigercat assigned to VMP-254 rests just off shore after a belly landing. The propeller of the right engine appears feathered, its blades turned into the air stream. This indicates that the engine probably malfunctioned in flight, perhaps leading to the emergency landing. (The Museum of Flight)

A veer to the right on landing sent this Bearcat into the island of Tarawa in August 1947. The fighter struck right wing first, nose digging into the deck. The aircraft then cartwheeled against the carrier's superstructure. Men above and down on the deck gawk at the wreck. A few even take a peek from the portholes nearest the stricken plane. (National Archives)

Just a few feet over the deck of Antietam, a too-quickly sinking Bearcat flyer gets into trouble. A quick burst of power from the engine has dangerously skewed the little fighter's altitude. At this point, it's unlikely the pilot will be able to recover. Note the sailors in the portside catwalk jumping onto the deck to sprint out of the way of the imperiled F8F. (National Museum of Naval Aviation)

Days before the fighting ended in Korea, Lt. Jerome Skyrud nearly met his end. The flyer from *Philippine Sea* was attacking targets near Tanchon, North Korea, when his F4U-4 was peppered by machine gun bullets and shrapnel. He elected to land on an emergency strip in South Korea instead of attempting to trap aboard ship. (Naval Historical Center)

This F6F-3 ditched in the ocean near San Diego on January 12, 1944. The Navy recovered the Hellcat in 1970, and eventually restored the rare fighter. The aircraft is now on display at the National Museum of Naval Aviation in Pensacola, Florida. (National Museum of Naval Aviation)

CLEAR THE DECK!

At the end of a long, long voyage, the anchor drops from the rusty, battered bow of the aircraft carrier Essex. *(U.S. Navy via Paul Madden)*

Index

Index

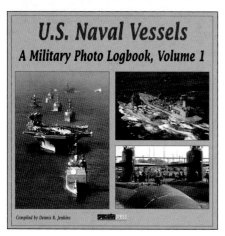
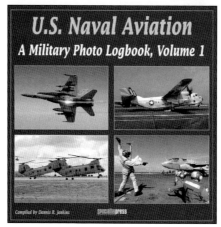
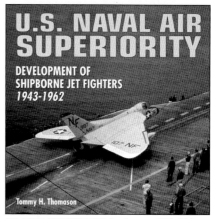

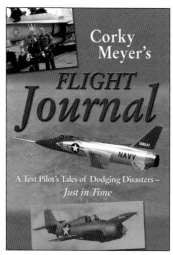